INFLUENCER FAST TRACK

~~~

From Zero to Influencer
in the next 6 Months!

10X Your Marketing & Branding for
Coaches, Consultants, Professionals
& Entrepreneurs

by Gundi Gabrielle

The following trademarks are owned by *Happy Dolphin Enterprises, LLC:* SassyZenGirl™, Influencer Fast Track™, Dream Clients On Autopilot™, The Sassy Way™, When You Have No Clue™, #ClaimYourFREEDOM™

Cover Design: Iram Shahzadi
Cover Photo: Lori Dorn

First Edition Paperback: May 2018

ISBN: 978-1982977115

The Cataloging-In-Publication Data is on file with the Library of Congress.

*This is a **SassyZenGirl** Guide*

Dedication

To the amazing teachers who showed me the way:

Jon Morrow, Evan Carmichael, Gary Vaynerchuk, Sean Ogle, Alex Becker, Chris M. Walker, John Lee Dumas, Pat Flynn, Richard Branson, Robert Kiyosaki, Tim Ferriss, Tony Robbins, Josh Steimle, Oprah Winfrey, Louise Hay, Russell Brunson, Richie Norton, Brian Dean, and Derek Sivers.

Some of you know me, some of you don't, but you all have made a tremendous difference in my life and helped me achieve freedom and fulfillment beyond my wildest dreams!

You showed me that marketing and running a business can be fun and how to do it smartly and successfully while helping and empowering others - and - adding a little sunshine to the world.

I will forever be grateful & and dedicate this little book to YOU!

An emphatic, Sassylicious WOW to you!
Gundi Gabrielle
aka SassyZenGirl – #ClaimYourFREEDOM

TABLE OF CONTENTS

Please Bookmark the RESOURCES PAGE
so you can access all tools and resources mentioned
throughout this book with direct links to each:

InfluencerFastTrack.com/Resources

So what...?

You have something awesome to share!

You know you can really make a difference in the world and help people. You have laid it all out, an amazing system, a method that works or an amazing product that you developed.

You are pumped and ready for action - bring it on!!

BUT then...

Total shocker...

NO ONE is interested, no matter how hard you try!

What the booty...?!

You know you need to up your marketing.

You know you should do more, but it's all very confusing.

You hate pitching and telling everyone about your business. Makes you seem desperate (YUK!).

Marketing feels overwhelming, against your natural instincts - and you don't really have time for it anyway.

You tried social media for a while, you *really* gave it a go, but that, too, was just tedious and time consuming and you still only have a handful of followers.

Why is no one listening? Why - *SassyDarn(!)* - is this so hard?

Why don't people just "find" you? Isn't that how it usually works? Someone gets lucky, gets "discovered"?

Just not you.

Nope.

Not happenin'...

You might as well give up - what's the point anyway?

Sound familiar?

Even just a little...?

If YES - then I welcome you to the FAST TRACK, because it definitely doesn't have to be this hard!

There is a straight path through the online jungle, a shortcut really, a fast track, and it's not that hard to learn.

"Knowledge is power" as they say, and knowledge is all that's between you and the success and recognition you deserve.

The reason why marketing seems so darn difficult and frustrating, is simply that you don't know what to do.

They gave you systems and step-by-step methods to guide you in whatever profession you learned, but somehow no one ever taught you "that marketing thing".

It all seems very vague and worst of all, it seems to depend on luck - or - vast sums of cash.

Maybe you don't have either, so it seems you are doomed?

Well... no. Not at all!

Marketing and growing a brand *can* be learned. There *are* step-by-step systems and proven methods to take your brand from little known to influencer famous - and it doesn't have to take years or cost thousands of greenies.

Really!

Best of all:

It can be FUN!

Yes, marketing *can* be fun and once you know what to do, what steps to take and when, you'll be flying in no time - *and* enjoy the ride.

What I will share with you in this book is a blueprint from:

ZERO = no followers or clients or only a few

to

**well-known, established AUTHORITY in your
field**

in just a few months - *IF* - you apply yourself.

That part is crucial, of course, and depends on how
much you want it, how *committed* you really are.

I can show you the way, but **you** have to walk it and if
you are ready, let's begin!

In case you are wondering: **WHO** is she to make such
promises? **WHY** should I even listen to her?

I hear ya. Fair questions.

Let's get that out of the way:

For starters, I was not "born" with a marketing gene
and I knew nothing about business until my mid 30s. I
actually started in music as a classical conductor,
organist, and pianist. I eventually ran my own music
company, a 200-member oratorio choir and orchestra
and we toured internationally, including performances
for the Pope and at Carnegie Hall.

I wore many "hats" in this new company, not just the music director. In fact, I wore *all* the hats, incl. booking and PR, and I loved every part of it!

I had no clue about marketing back then, but still somehow managed to book our brand new ensemble to some of the most famous venues in the world and - fill those venues, usually with a standing ovation to boot.

I'm not sharing this to brag, no worries, but because I used some of the same marketing hacks that I will share with you in this book. They cost no money. We were not famous when we started. Most of it came about through networking and what I call OPA (more on that later).

I even filled Carnegie Hall without a marketing budget - on a weeknight no less, in February of 2012 - and not by some magic hack or famous connections, but by building relationships with peers and institutions and coming up with win-win opportunities for everyone involved.

Conducting *Bach's B Minor Mass* at Carnegie Hall was one of the greatest days of my life and not just for me, but for everyone involved.

It was an incredible evening.

Even the audience seemed to feel it and stayed for an astounding 20 minutes of standing ovations for an

ensemble they had never heard of and with long home commutes still ahead.

As a long-time New Yorker, I'm used to people rushing out during the last note, but not that night. There was something special, and we all shared in it.

Had I been scared by the magnitude of this adventure, scared by all the marketing involved and how to fill the place, this would have never happened.

Like I said, I knew nothing about online marketing back then, not even social media. Nada! And yet, it was still possible, with passion, enthusiasm, and the belief that it could be done.

If your dreams don't scare you, they are too small.
Richard Branson

If I can do it, so can you!

Maybe not Carnegie Hall, but something else awesome that you always wanted to do.

If you are reading this book, then you probably have a dream and something amazing to share. It's bursting within you, but you don't know how to reach people.

It's frustrating and devastating at times, but there is hope on the horizon and light at the end of the tunnel. Just bear with me...

What else qualifies me to write this book?

A number of things, but mainly, I wanted freedom. Freedom to travel, freedom financially, freedom to choose.

I searched around the internet, started with blogging and eventually found my path in self-publishing. I published a couple of #1 Bestsellers, reached the top 100 of business authors, and most of all, was able to build a platform and six-figure income, mostly passive, through books and courses and various other businesses.

I *did* learn marketing eventually, and I've come to really enjoy it!

I've also connected with some truly amazing people and observed their path to the top.

Out of that came this book and it *will* show you a fast track to influencer success that is amazing, fun and inspiring.

Ethical and legit. No scammy business, and something that you will find truly rewarding, no matter what field you are in.

I'm so excited to share this with you! And I hope I can help you short cut the process.

What I have done, anyone can do. Really!

It may not seem that way right now, but once you finish this book, you will feel confident and empowered that you - yes, YOU! - can reach your dream and share with the world all the awesome you have to offer! And it doesn't have to take years or cost loads of money!

While I prefer a quiet life to the spotlight these days - I had enough dazzle during my music days - I *do* know how to make it happen and have certainly created the freedom that I always wanted and the ability to share with people all around the world. That is truly priceless and the greatest gift of all!

I look forward to seeing you rise to your full AWEsomeness over the next year and can't wait to hear your stories!

With that, let's get started and dive right in with:

Part 1

What makes an Influencer?

What indeed?

Let's get "pumped" with Wikipedia's definition:

"Influencer marketing is a form of marketing in which focus is placed on influential people rather than the target market as a whole. It identifies the individuals that have influence over potential buyers, and orients marketing activities around these influencers."

Sounds a bit stuffy, but offers a few good points.

Most people think of *social media* when they hear "influencer". Instagram in particular, but that is just one segment.

While influencers usually have a large social media following, it isn't necessarily the platform they are famous for. They could just as well be an influential:

- *podcaster*
- *author*
- *blogger*
- *entrepreneur*
- *coach/trainer*
- *movie star*
- *athlete*
- *musician*

and many more.

The **three INGREDIENTS** they all have in common are:

#1 - Authority
= perceived as one of the **top experts** in their field — among the best of the best.

#2 - Following
= a large, **loyal following** trusting their advice and following their suggestions, be it actions or purchase decisions.

#3 - Success
= impressive **results**, both **professionally** and **financially**. Someone to look up to and learn from.

That's the target!

Easy enough, right...?

Well, not at first sight, of course, and before I show you the good stuff, let's dispel a few myths about influencer stardom:

Influencer Myths

#1 - It takes years to become an influencer.

#2 - It is very expensive (marketing, production, PR).

#3 - It is mostly luck and cannot be planned.

#4 - You need to be "discovered".

#5 - Marketing is difficult.

#6 - You have to become world famous.

#7 - You have to be extraordinarily talented.

#8 - You need awesome tech skills.

#9 - You need to be attractive.

#10 - You need to be young (ideally in your 20s).

...and probably a few more.

Out of the above, which ones do you believe? Are there a few that have prevented you from taking action, because you thought it could never work anyway?

Make a list and keep it handy. As we go through this book, you will see them dispelled one by one and you will realize that you (yes, you!) can become an influencer, even within the next six months!

WOW!

"Is this a scam?" - you might wonder and the answer is an emphatic "No"! Definitely not.

Give me an hour of your time and I will show you why.

First of all, "Influencer" does not mean you have to be world famous. Not at all.

"Influence" usually relates to a specific niche, and your audience does not have to be in the millions.

Russell Brunson, one of the most famous marketers and entrepreneurs of our day, made an interesting observation in this regard:

He described how people at his church who had heard that he was "rather successful" *(to put it mildly)*, asked him whether he was "famous". He replied: Oh no, just "internet famous". "Real famous" would not be fun. I'm paraphrasing, but you get the gist.

While Russell is a famous figure and one of the biggest influencers in the world of online marketing and business, the average person on the street would probably not know his name.

They will know Oprah or Richard Branson, but most influencers are known only to a specific target audience.

They most certainly have influence among that audience, but they are not world famous.

While Russell is, of course, one of the big guns, there are many so-called micro-influencers who have a much smaller, very targeted audience, but that audience is absolutely loyal and will listen to everything they say.

So...

You don't have to become the next Oprah or Tony Robbins. Though...who knows?...you might!
But you *can* rise to "influencer" level and make a good, fulfilling living - without being known by millions.

I hope that takes the pressure off a little, and with that, let's look at the biggest worry most people have: the ominous "M-word". Yep, Marketing!

Do you need to be a Marketing Genius?

No, thankfully not, but there *is* a learning curve. Not rocket science and *much* easier than most things you learned in college or even high school, but it does involve some learning and certainly commitment and effort.

Not exactly a shocker.

The good part: if you employ some of the techniques I will share in part 2, you can quickly start earning money while you learn and take the first steps to becoming an influencer.

Try that with college!

Plus, the results will come much faster, sometimes instantly, and with much less expense than a college education.

The first important step is a shift in mindset.

A paradigm shift, really:

No matter what your background: as an influencer, even in the making, you are now an entrepreneur!

Congrats! Whether you like it or not, you *are* - or you'd better be.

In this venture you are not waiting for a boss to tell you what to do. You are not slaving away for a paycheck. You are free to decide whatever you want, and you need to **own** that freedom.

The most important skill for any entrepreneur is marketing.

Yep, the "M-word" as I call it, and if you have issues with "M" (and most people do), I invite you to read this humorous article I wrote a while back called:

"How to Chill with the M-Word"

Marketing is not difficult, and it does not have to be tedious or unpleasant.

It also has nothing to do with being sleazy or salesy - quite the opposite. Instead, smart marketing is built on these five pillars:

1) **CARE** for your customers, be it your followers, readers or clients.

2) Provide what people **urgently NEED** (market research).

3) Build long-term **RELATIONSHIPS.**

4) Leverage **OPA** (other people's audiences): peers, influencers, institutions, etc.

5) Be **YOU**! (aka awesome, unique branding)

Doesn't sound so bad, right?

You could do that even if you are an introvert *(I'm, too, by the way)* and were not born with a marketing gene?

Marketing is only scary if you don't know what to do, and this book will get you started and fast track the process.

Speaking of fast track:

Let's look at the **3 FAST TRACK FACTORS** that everyone has access to and that will make what may seem out of reach, surprisingly easy and doable:

The 3 Influencer FAST TRACK Factors

FACTOR #1 : Internet Magic

The internet has changed our lives dramatically, removed gatekeepers and put power back into the hands of the people - all of us.

I remember back in the '90s, your best chances of creating passive income were MLM and real estate. The internet was still in its infancy (*as were cell phones - can you believe it?*)

Fast forward to this day and it has become incredibly easy to connect with people all around the world within seconds. Social media platforms, forums, groups, reddits, and chat rooms have put billions of people in your potential reach and dramatically changed even the political landscape in some cases.

Friends, peers, potential customers, and even influencers are just a tweet, comment, or email away.

We are so used to this sheer unlimited networking potential that we often forget how incredible it really is, and that it's still a pretty new phenomenon!

In addition to connecting and networking, the internet has "blessed" us with a whole new form of products and by extension, passive income potentials:

Digital products

Be it e-books, online courses, softwares or apps, digital products have made it *so* much easier and less expensive to start a business without having to worry about supplies, assembly, staff or shipping, opening a whole new world of passive income streams that would have been unthinkable even 10 years ago.

Not only that, in tandem with these new product types, e-commerce platforms have made a formidable appearance and have changed how we live and do business forever.

When you sell a product or service through platforms like:

- *Amazon*
- *eBay*
- *Fiverr*
- *Udemy*
- *Etsy*
- *iTunes*
- *Shopify*

or share your free content on:

- *Medium*
- *YouTube*
- *iTunes (podcasts)*

you are *leveraging* the huge, worldwide audiences these platforms have built over years - much vaster than you could ever reach with your own website.

If you learn how to rank on each, meaning how to get your products to show at the top of the search results through "search engine optimization" (aka "SEO"), you can generate an unlimited, evergreen traffic to whatever you sell or offer, pretty much on autopilot.

SEO hacks for each platform can be learned. Ranking in the top spots is not luck! There are step-by-step systems, and they don't require a PhD to implement.

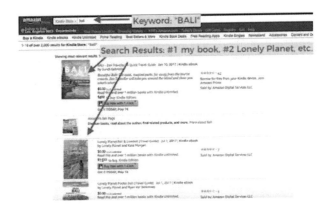

Of course, leverage is not limited to platforms.

A tweet or an email from an influencer can massively drive traffic to your business, products, or services in a matter of hours.

In the olden days, that would have required a TV or radio appearance - both limited by region - or a review in a major publication. Both would have given you a short-term burst, quickly followed by oblivion, buried in dusty archives, never to be seen again.

Expensive ads were another option but were also limited in both scope and time. Certainly nothing like the vast, instant reach of the internet, and I haven't even mentioned social media platforms...

Of course, you know all this, and yet many business owners are not leveraging or fully grasping how truly powerful and amazing these potentials are and how it can drastically speed up the growth of any business and influencer status.

The Power of Leverage

You might remember the real estate investing term "**OPM**" (= other people's money), meaning:

Use (leverage) other people's money (banks, investors, tenants) to grow your real estate empire exponentially faster than you ever could with just your own funds.

In a similar vein and much less risky, the internet has expanded "**OPA**" (= other people's audiences).

Meaning:

When a peer or influencer shares your product, service or business with their large audience, you are *leveraging* the trust they built with their followers over many years to promote *your* products, including your books.

Usually, this is a two-way street. With peers an exchange, with influencers you might offer something to make it worth their while, such as a mention in your book or an awesome new hack you will implement for free that will greatly benefit their business.

The same goes for institutions and organizations, especially once they include you in their "Recommended Resources" section, resulting in evergreen traffic and marketing for your brand.

OPA is free PR and often massively effective, especially with large influencers or institutions.

OPA "on Steroids"

Leveraging the gigantic, worldwide audiences of platforms like Amazon, eBay or iTunes is pretty much **OPA "on steroids"** IF you know how to get ranked there and keep selling long-term.

This brings us to **FAST TRACK FACTOR #2**, the magic Bullet of this entire blueprint:

FACTOR #2 – Bestseller Magic

Bestseller Publishing, as I call it, can be the absolute fastest way to add the three ingredients of Influencer status:

- *Authority:* clout and prestige of a top expert
- *Following:* large, loyal audience
- *Success:* impressive results

Best of all: traffic is instant.

Literally right from launch day!

I don't know of any other marketing strategy that comes even close!

Before we go into the why and how, let's first address a few concerns you might have about publishing (and no, this is not a book about Kindle publishing, but <u>how to incorporate</u> the power of publishing to fast track everything else):

- *It takes months or years to write a book.*
- *You need a publishing deal.*
- *It's expensive to self-publish.*
- *All my topics have already been covered.*
- *Too much competition.*
- *I'm hopeless at marketing.*
- *I'm not a writer.*
- *Will people like my book?*

Anything else?

The short answer:

None of these are true!

How do I know?

Because when I first started in late 2015, I was not a writer, had zero online marketing experience and no following. Zip!

I had seen people publish bestsellers on Amazon and somehow got it into my head that I wanted that #1 Amazon Bestseller badge.

I went about finding someone who could teach me, someone who had published multiple #1 Bestsellers, not a theorist, and followed her guidance - every single step - to the letter.

I was shocked, but 30 days later, I had my first #1 Bestseller and started making about $1,000 to $1,500 per month on autopilot!

I started my international travels soon after, and thanks to low living expenses in other countries, this little book pretty much sustained me during my first year *and* kept sending me a continuous stream of new subscribers and social media followers almost daily!!

From DAY ONE!

30 days may seem extreme, but my first book was a simple how-to book on starting a blog, a topic I knew inside out and could easily write down in a week. Plus, I wasn't working a full-time job and could focus all my time on this new venture.

If you have a busy job and family life, give it 90 days, but that time frame is definitely doable if you apply yourself.

Keep in mind that Kindle books are usually not very long. In fact, "short is the new long", with readers clearly preferring shorter books in a series than one big chunk.

A good average length is 15,000 to 30,000 words, and since you will be an expert on your topic, you can easily complete your first book in a month for just the writing portion.

You can also compile your best blog posts and tie them together to a well flowing book, making this even easier.

Or employ a ghostwriter, though I would not recommend this strategy, except in rare cases, because the key to all this lies in *you* connecting with your readers (directly, not through someone else).

I hope you can see now that publishing a nonfiction book is not a herculean task, but can easily be achieved within the next 30 to 90 days. For marketing, there is a proven, simple, step-by-step system that can easily get you to bestseller status, possibly even a #1 Bestseller.

None of it is rocket science or terribly time consuming. You just need a blueprint that works and in the free training video below I will show you the exact steps I take to launch all my books to #1 - and - keep them selling long-term. That is, by the way, the area most self-published authors struggle with: keeping books selling past the first launch and that is, of course, crucial for your influencer success and everything else we will discuss in this book.

FREE 1 hour Training Video:

"7 STEPS to YOUR FIRST #1 BESTSELLER!"

Access at: InfluencerFastTrack.com

Did it cost much?

No, usually not more than $500 per book and that includes cover, proofreader and launch week promos.

Try that with Facebook ads!

Or SEO for your website.

Or starting any other business.

What about competition?

High competition is good! The more popular, the better, as long as you understand how Amazon's ranking algorithm works, optimize your books accordingly, and execute a "power launch". None of it terribly difficult as you will see in the video.

What about traditional publishing?

Unless you are world famous with a huge following, a traditional publisher is a terrible idea.

Why?

Because:

- You will lose the rights to your books.
- It takes a long time from contract to publish, usually
- at least a year.
- These days publishers still expect you - <u>and won't sign you</u> - unless you already have a huge following (minimum 10K followers). They will expect *you* to do most of the marketing, so if you thought a traditional publisher would save you from "M" - think again!

- Even famous authors like Tim Ferriss and Gary Vaynerchuk carefully plan out their launches and are fully involved in the marketing.
- Traditional book royalties are small in comparison.

Unless you have a huge following already, you are *much* better off self-publishing, and if you *have* a huge following, you might as well publish yourself and keep the 70% royalty.

That is what Amazon pays for most Kindle books (depending on book price), plus 60% minus production costs for paperback or "POD" (= print-on-demand).

❖ ❖ ❖ ❖ ❖ ❖ ❖

Now that we have addressed concerns and objections, let's turn to **WHY** *Bestseller Publishing* is the crucial keystone of this INFLUENCER blueprint - the FAST TRACK magic that makes it so awesome:

#1 - The prestige of a bestselling author

Remember **AUTHORITY?**

Influencer ingredient #1?

Nothing matches the credibility and respect of "Bestselling Author" status or even "#1 Bestselling author"!

Add that to your signature, and you are immediately perceived in a different league, a top expert, and, yes, an "influencer"!

Whether true or not, people will assume that you are. Two little words making all the difference!

They will also expect premium prices and even a waiting list for your services and products.

Tell me any other marketing method that can get you there so quickly - instantly, really!

=> Instant Influencer Magic!

#2 - Grow a following on autopilot

Influencer ingredient #2: A loyal following *(subscribers and social media followers).*

A best-selling book can send you a continuous stream of new subscribers and social media followers completely on autopilot.

People who love your book will naturally want to follow you elsewhere. You just have to tell them how and where. We will cover the how in STEP 2 during the second half of this book.

As long as your books keep selling well, you can expect a regular stream of traffic to any platform or outlet you choose.

That also includes your podcast, YouTube channel, Blog, e-commerce store and, of course, any services or products you offer.

Instantly.

As soon as you launch!

And mostly free!

You might employ Amazon ads (AMS) for long term sales, but they cost a pittance compared to Facebook ads, SEO or Google ads.

You also might run a promo occasionally - anywhere between $5 to $110.

Again, nothing compared to other ad expenses.

Best of all:

Amazon _pays you_ to grow your brand, get new followers and clients on autopilot and build your influencer status!

That's right!

If your books sell well, you will also enjoy a continuous stream of passive income in the form of royalties.

And...

potentially affiliate income - more on that later.

#3 - Turn cold prospects into ardent fans and replace your sales pitch

Books allow you to present your expertise and awesomeness in a non-salesy way. If you write the best book on the topic and provide phenomenal value, readers will be _dying_ to work with you or check out your products. And, as I pointed out before, they will expect to pay premium rates, even be grateful if you can fit them in.

Most importantly, you started building a relationship with them. Readers feel like they know you and just had a conversation with you through your books. That kind of trust and respect is priceless. The greatest copywriter in the world couldn't match that.

Which brings us to:

#4 - Relationship marketing on autopilot

Relationship marketing is the new, "cool" marketing method of our day and crucial for any influencer.

> *The Greatest Marketing Method Ever: CARE!*
> *Gary Vaynerchuk*

What do I mean?

Rather than seeing nothing but dollar signs in your clients and followers, focus on building relationships. Take an interest. Ask them what they need and what they are struggling with.

Not only does it provide you with a gold mine of information that you can turn into content and products, but more importantly, relationship marketing allows you to build a loyal and passionate fan base that will follow you for years to come and *trust* your advice and direction.

=> the second crucial ingredient for influencer status! (More on that in STEP 3).

First, though, let's check out **FACTOR #3** in this trilogy:

FACTOR #3 - Funnel Magic

What is a funnel?

Excellent question! - and a crucial one for understanding this book and how successful online marketing works.

A sales funnel is a chain of products that lead a customer (and that includes readers of your books) to your brand and products with the least resistance.

In fact, sales funnels often start with a free product.

If you include a free offer (free cheat sheet, checklist) in your books to get subscribers for your mailing list, this will be a part of your funnel.

Why?

Because you can then build a relationship with your new subscribers and introduce them to other, higher priced products.

You probably heard of "FREE, plus Shipping"?

Same concept. The word "free" is irresistible and _the_ most powerful marketing trigger in any language.

You can find more trigger words in my article "_Words that Sell._"

Ironically, merchants who use the "FREE, plus Shipping" method often make tens of thousands of dollars, because they set the shipping price much higher than the actual postage fees. It's called a "handling fee" and often two to three times higher than the basic shipping cost.

Customers know this and yet are willing - even eager - to pay $9.95 for "shipping & handling" as long as the product is free - even if that product is worth less than $9.95!

Mind-blowing but proven many times and shows how irresistible and powerful free offers are.

Smart book marketers usually have at least one permafree (permanently free) book as a lead magnet to draw new readers in.

If those readers like the free book, they will usually buy more books by this author and gladly pay a higher price because they are now convinced that they will get the desired help and results.

No more pitching or clever sales copy needed!

Give a free taste, provide *awesome* value and then offer more.

That's how simple smart marketing really is.

The next step in a sales funnel is usually a low-priced product called **"Tripwire"**. $4.97 or $7.99 are typical price points.

Your paid Kindle books fit that bill perfectly and sales psychology tells us that once someone buys from you, even at a very low price, they are now much more likely to also buy higher priced items.

The initial barrier is gone. That difficult first sale was converted. From now on, things will get a lot easier.

While your Kindle books are low priced, they still show a commitment from your buyer to invest in an author unknown to them and not return the item.

In fact, they might even give you a glowing review!

As successful authors, **Part #1** and **Part #2** of a classic sales funnel have already been completed!

Halfway there!

What remains are:

#3 - A CORE PRODUCT (or several). Something in a medium price range, anywhere from $27 to $297 depending on your niche and topic.
Please note: pricing varies greatly between niches, and these are just rough numbers to give you an idea.

#4 - A PREMIUM PRODUCT in the $497 to $1997 range (or higher in some niches) - again, not limited to just one.

Core and premium products can include online courses, but also services, coaching, consulting, and any other products.

The second half of this book will go over many different options for #3 and #4 and how to implement them in phases as you grow your brand.

Before we go there, let me share one more fast-track ingredient. The one most overlooked of all:

The *SECRET INGREDIENT*

The one activity that will increase your influencer growth tenfold, more than anything else, aside from publishing, is networking and cultivating relationships.

What do I mean?

We already talked about the power of leverage. The more you build relationships and connect with people, that is:

- see competitors as opportunities for collaboration, rather than enemies

and

- customers as partners and friends that you help, but who are also helping <u>you</u>, both to grow your brand and by giving you feedback,

the faster you will grow.

As the saying goes:

It is not so much *what* you know, but *who* you know and once you truly understand and *cherish* the awesome power of leverage, you can grow and expand at amazing speeds. And at a fraction of conventional marketing costs.

Relationships cover all parts of your business and we will address them as we go through the seven STEPS, but here is a first look:

- *Your peers, including competitors*
- *Your audience, customers, clients, readers, students*
- *Influencers, big and small*
- *Institutions, relevant to your niche*
- *Major platforms to share your products*

With that...

Let's rock it with the **7-STEP FORMULA** aka **The INFLUENCER FAST TRACK**:

Part 2

The 7-STEP FORMULA

Six *months...?!*

...was probably your first reaction when you saw this cover. *Is this a marketing gimmick or is she for real?*

The short answer is: YES, it is possible, but it also depends on a number of obvious factors like:

- *your niche*
- *how much time you have*
- *how far along you already are*
- *how much you already applied some of the steps*
- *how committed and determined you are(!)*

and a few others.

There is never a guarantee, but the bottom line is: even as a complete newbie, if you have the time and the determination *(that part is very important!)*, you can make it happen in six months. Definitely 12!

Will you be world famous and make millions? Probably not, but that's not what defines an influencer as we saw earlier.

Can you grow a loyal following and become recognized within your field beyond just a small regional reach? Recognized enough that a significant number of people in your niche will know your name?

Absolutely!

And that is what this book will show you. Beyond that, you can scale it up as much as you want. It's mostly rinse and repeat at that point, but you first need to get there, and this book will show you how.

A 6 month timeline could look something like this:

Months 1-2: STEPS 1-3

Months 3-5: add STEPS 4-5, *while continuing 2 and 3*

Month 6: continue STEPS 2-5 and add STEP 6

After 6 months: add STEP 7

This timeline will make more sense once you have gone through the 7 STEPS, and it's certainly not set in stone. This is just *one* example of how it *can* be done. For most people, 12 months will be more realistic, especially if you have a busy life already.

I would recommend reading through this book at least once to get an overview and then lay out a 6 or 12-month plan that can work with your unique situation.

Be sure to bookmark the **Resources Page** *(no optin required)* with a listing of all the tools and resources mentioned throughout this book:

InfluencerFastTrack.com/Resources

Having a timeline and milestones to meet will focus your efforts and keep you on track. If it takes a little longer or things turn out differently, no biggie, you simply adjust and set a new timeline as you go along.

Just lay something out and follow it as best you can. You'll get there a lot faster and it's easier to measure success.

Whatever timeline you choose, this formula will help you to gradually increase your:

AUTHORITY
FOLLOWING
SUCCESS

the three main ingredients of influencer status.

Let's begin!

STEP 1:
The "Goosebump Factor"

Make it a No-Brainer!

The "Goosebump Factor" aka Branding!

This is where it all starts, where you lay the foundation and where you

Design an IRRESISTIBLE BRAND!

I know, sounds really complicated, but let's break it down:

An irresistible, clearly defined brand that people will love and identify with, is composed of the following **five GOODIES**:

#1 - A marketable **sub niche** that you can dominate, where you become the go-to person that everyone refers to.

#2 - A clearly defined target **audience.** *(Hint: it's never "everybody.")*

#3 - A unique **benefit** that only *your* brand can provide and better than anyone else.

#4 - An **"It" factor** that makes it fun and irresistible to be a part of your brand.

#5 - A memorable **story** that your audience can identify with, that defines you, and how your brand came about.

Let's look at each in detail:

#1 - Marketable SUB NICHE

This is one of the most crucial elements to influencer success and the one most often overlooked.

Let me give you an example:

Let's say you are trying to quit smoking. You tried for years and nothing works. You also tried visualization and even worked with a success coach, but somehow it just doesn't stick. You have some success, you last for a while and then you fall off the wagon again.

Two of your friends have tackled the problem successfully. You meet them for dinner one night and both share enthusiastically how their coaches got them over the finish line. Peter worked with a life coach named Chris and it took him six months. Mary only started a few weeks ago, but she was already able to quit. Mary worked with Phil, known as the "Quit Smoking Coach", and his methods seem to be totally amazing.

Both rave about their coaches, both seem to be successful, and maybe Mary is just more disciplined. Either way, who would you choose as your coach?

The answer is obvious: The Quit Smoking Coach, and not just because Mary achieved her goal faster. After all, she might have just been more determined or less addicted.

No, the part that's irresistible and makes this a no-brainer is the fact that Phil is a *specialist* in *exactly* the area you need help with.

Even if there wasn't a success story with Quit Smoking Phil, even if Mary had not succeeded, the mere fact that Phil was laser-specialized would have always given him the edge.

Hard to explain, but that's how we are wired.

A specialist exudes exclusivity and excellence. Premium quality, VIP.

A generalist, a jack of all trades, seems common in comparison. The bar seems much lower, and you can't reach the same excellence in multiple areas as you can when focusing on just one.

Simple physics.

A specialist can apply laser focus to one thing and one thing only. He or she can focus all their formidable energy on becoming the best of the best in that one field.

The fast track - and really a must-have requirement for influencer success - is for you to find a sub niche, a specialty, that you can dominate. Where you are perceived the top expert and go-to person that all the generalists refer to.

Make sense?

How do you find your sub niche?

Ideally, you already know your field quite well. If not, it's high time to find out:

Start by subscribing to at least 10 top influencers in your field. Their blog, podcast, YouTube channel, or whatever their biggest platform is.

Spend some time, at least a week or two going through all their content and, very importantly, all the comments. Comments can give you a gold mine of information because they often share frustrations, things that readers wish was available, problems they face, and the specific language they use.

Make note of everything and watch for trends. If they use specific phrases, write them down. They will be great for your sales copy later on. Also, take note of objections and common myths you find.

Finally, compile a list of topics and areas that haven't really been explored yet, where you could leave your mark.

Comments on forums, social media platforms, and reddit threads will also be helpful.

You want to get into the head of your potential followers, clients, and customers.

What keeps them up at night? What would they give anything if someone could solve it for them?

What influencers do they like and why? Check those influencers out too and repeat the process.

Same with bestselling books. Whatever medium you most prefer. Do this for about two weeks without making any decisions.

You will notice over time how your ideas and perceptions will change and how you gain a much better understanding of what people actually *want* versus what you *think* they want.

Smart entrepreneurs *(and as a budding influencer, you are most certainly an entrepreneur now)* reverse-engineer the process. They find out what people most urgently need and then provide it.

Much simpler and more effective.

Pay attention to what people care about and reverse-engineer it.
Gary Vaynerchuk

This in-depth research and understanding of your audience and niche will make all the difference in your long-term success.

To see what's currently trending you can check your niche in **Buzzsumo** *(most shared articles at any given time)* or curation sites like Alltop and Medium. Again, read the comments and related articles.

By the end of two weeks you should have a short list of possible sub niches that you know will be of interest and could generate a following.

Now you need to check whether that niche is marketable. Can you make money with it? Are people willing to pay for books, courses, etc.?

An easy way to find out is Google:

Google your **[your sub niche candidates]** + "buy" one by one.

You should see a lot of product results and ads. If you don't, it usually means that people might like the niche, but aren't willing to spend money, want everything for free. Obviously not a good choice, unless you don't want to monetize your influencer status.

You also want to check the number of search results to make sure there is at least reasonable traffic.

If you have access to the *Google Keyword Planner* you can get a rough estimate of monthly searches. They no longer give exact numbers unless you book a campaign, but a rough number is all you need here, meaning:

Keyword (by relevance)	Avg. monthly searches	Competition	Ad impression share	Top of page bid (low range)	Top of page bid (high range)
cat toys	10K – 100K	High	–	$0.85	$3.25
best cat toys	1K – 10K	High	–	$0.46	$3.25
kitten toys	1K – 10K	High	–	$1.22	$2.54
interactive cat toys	1K – 10K	High	–	$0.86	$4.21
cat accessories	1K – 10K	High	–	$0.97	$2.12
cool cat toys	100 – 1K	High	–	$1.30	$3.25

This will give you a general sense of how much interest there is in your niche. How many people are searching for it each month.

The video on the **Resources page** will show you how to set up the Google Keyword Planner.

Ideally, you are looking for a popular overall niche (weight loss, dog training, etc.) and a sub niche within that bigger niche with little to no influencers, but reasonable traffic. That's where you can make your mark quite easily.

After validating your candidates for marketability, you are now ready to pick your final winner - congrats!

CAVEAT: Research can seem tedious and you might be tempted to skip this part, but if you do, it will be *very* difficult to stand out and unless you stand out, why would anyone follow you? Just look at it from an audience's perspective.

You can employ all the marketing tactics in the world, but if you don't offer what people *want* or there is too much competition because you are too general - it won't make an ounce of difference.

The more thoroughly you do this step, the easier (and less expensive) your marketing will be - and for a long time to come.

Instead, make it fun!

You obviously love your niche or you wouldn't be in it. So make this exploration an exciting **ADVENTURE** - *one of my favorite words* - and find out what's going on, what audiences are saying and how you could make a *real* difference in their lives.

How awesome will it be when you can truly do that, really inspire and help someone and change their lives? And gain money and freedom in the process?

The more **FUN** - *another favorite word of mine* - you have with this, the more future audiences will LOVE to be around you. Enthusiasm is contagious and irresistible. So, go, have fun!

#2 - Target Audience

While you research your niche, you will also gain a better understanding of your target audience and that will be another crucial ingredient for influencer success. If you don't know who you are targeting, how can you possibly find the best ways to reach them?

Make sense?

It's never everybody and the better you understand your audience, the easier it will be to connect with them.

Now is the time to create your **Audience AVATAR** (usually called a "customer" or "client avatar").

This will vary greatly depending on your sub niche. In some cases it will be clear by gender, age group or other demographics.

Often though it will be other characteristics like personality, specific talents or lack thereof, pain points or frustrations.

Again, don't make it a tedious exercise. Have fun with this:

Create a real bio, complete with photo and name.

Just pick a name you like and then Google that name and look at the images.

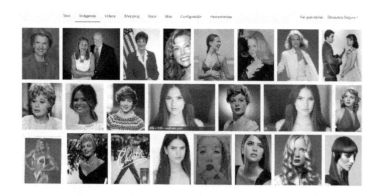

Why?

Because as you scroll through the images you will notice that some will draw you in. You just "like" that person even though you've never met them, but you still *feel* a connection.

That's what you are looking for. Someone you connect with who is representative of your audience.

Take some time and pick several if you want. Male/female, different age groups - whatever is relevant in your field.

Then print them out and start writing a (fictional) bio about that person. One typical for your audience.

If you feel silly about this, just bear with me, you will soon see the magic...

Once you are finished, "talk" to that image and avatar and ask them: would "Michael" like your brand / your product / your book? Would he relate to it? Would he understand it? Are you speaking his "language"? Does it solve his problem?

What objections might Julie have? What questions?

When you write your next blog post, write it to Julie. Have a conversation with her as you share your information.

Or Sally or Martin or whatever name you give your avatar(s).

Do you notice a difference?

Do you see how much more *specific* you become? Both in the way you write and the content you choose?

It makes all the difference in the world and the magic word is once again "specific" - just like "specialist".

Laser focus.

What you share and how you share it is no longer vague and general, but directed at your *unique* audience using the specific language *they* understand and like.

From now on, every time you create a new product, service or content, including a book, have a "conversation" with your avatar and get their feedback.

When you "talk" to a specific person - even a fictional one - everything you do will become laser targeted to that avatar, and your audience will feel like you are talking directly to them. They will feel like they know you and just had a conversation with you. That you understand them and *hear* them.

Out of that connection can grow a long-term, loyal relationship with followers who listen to your advice and choose *you* over everyone else - even if you are more expensive.

THAT - is magic!

Your avatar should obviously have the main frustrations, pain points and positive triggers as your target audience, the one you researched before.

Remember the comments? Have your avatar "say" them to you and then find ways to help them and solve their problems.

Only when your readers feel that you understand them, that you "*get*" them, will they follow you, listen to you and become an ardent fan of your brand.

#3 - Unique Benefit

Your unique benefit or "UVP" (= unique value proposition) as it's called in marketing cool will naturally develop out of #1 and #2.

If you spent the time to get to know your audience and what they most urgently need from you, this should be pretty easy. You should also have a good idea of what your peers offer and what is still lacking. Where you could provide a unique solution or a unique angle that can't be found anywhere else.

Out of that UVP, you want to craft your "elevator pitch": 1-2 concise sentences that describe what unique BENEFIT you are providing, *who* it is for and *why only you* can provide it.

Notice I said "**BENEFIT**", not: list of your features. Your audience is not interested in a list of products or features. They want to know - ideally in 10 seconds - what <u>benefit</u> they will gain from listening to you. How their lives will change and become easier through whatever help you offer. You need to "paint" a picture that touches them emotionally.

Answer that and most of all, evoke the *feeling* of how their lives will change, what it will *feel* like after your product or service has helped them, and you will have a good shot at capturing their interest.

Buying decisions are rarely rational, they are emotional. Plenty of studies have proven that. "Selling" people on following you, is also a "buying" decision even if no money is exchanged. The principle is the same.

You are asking complete strangers to take an interest in you and your offerings. To trust you and take your advice.

You have to "sell" them on that idea, just like with any other transaction.

Does not have to be unpleasant, sleazy or annoying. Not at all.

That's why we are doing all this research: to find out **who** your audience actually is and **what** they urgently need and want. Also, what they like and respond to.

Then - give it to them. Simple enough - or so it seems...

Having what people urgently want is the first important step.

Connecting with them in a way that's not pitchy or salesy, but rather makes them *feel* that you understand them, care and have a real solution, is the fast track to growing followers at rapid speed.

The article on the Resources Page will show you 25 awesome UVPs to get you going.

#4 - The "IT" Factor

To keep people excited and have them follow you regularly, your brand needs to have an "IT" factor - whatever that may be for your niche.

A specific look and feel. Your style, how you talk, how you communicate.

Do you have some brand specific lingo? colors? A mascot?

Do you have a cool name for your followers? One they will love to identify with?

Does not have to be extraordinary and very much depends on your overall niche, but start feeling your way into this. It will develop over time and you will probably make changes and adjustments, but start from day 1.

And...ask your audience for feedback. Let them choose occasionally when you pick a mascot or a name or logo, for example.

People *love* to share their opinion and it's a great way to get them engaged both with you and others in the community.

It also shows that you value their opinion, that they are important to you and - that you *listen*.

Once they feel that they are building something awesome *with* you. That they are part of a greater movement and their input is important and very much heard, they will become passionate ambassadors for your brand and be excited to share the journey.

Meaning: enthusiastically share your brand with their friends and colleagues, share your articles on social media, become affiliates to your products and maybe even open a door for you, like an influencer connection you didn't have before.

Six degrees of separation: The more you interact with your followers, get them excited to be a part of your brand and show them how much you appreciate them, the more you'll be amazed at the benefits and connections that can come to *you* through *their* connections and friends.

Most of all:

Follow your heart. **The "Goosebump Factor"** as I call it.

If *you* don't have goosebumps whenever you think of your brand, neither will anyone else.

It is your most reliable validator!

#5 - Your Story

Finally, your stories. Stories are pure magic and you need at least one to start.

Stories is what draws people in, what makes you unique. What makes them remember you.

"The guy who did....." "The girl who went through..... and then....."

They might not remember who you are and what you do in the beginning, but they *will* remember your story.

Think back to "Quit Smoking Phil" :

Not a very original story and still - you will probably remember it for a long time or at least the message of the story => the importance of being a specialist, rather than a jack-of-all-trades.

For your brand to become unique, it needs to be "YOU"!

Genuine, awesome, unique you - no cookie-cutter or platitudes. And certainly not perfect.

Nothing is more boring than perfect!

Really!

Instead, the unique, multi-faceted and sometimes flawed human being that you are - that we *all* are. That is who people can identify with and that is who they will follow.

You might have heard of the "Hero's Journey". It goes something like this:

- *Hero lives a normal life.*
- *A dramatic event turns hero's life upside down.*
- *Hero tries everything, but can't get him/herself out until...*
- *He/she meets a unique mentor (or method) that changes his/her paradigm to the core.*
- *Out of the ashes hero arises with a completely new outlook and solution to life and his/her specific problem.*
- *Hero finds joy and success again - bigger than ever before - and can now help YOU do the same.*
- *Enter: hero's unique method, product, message, book - you name it.*

If the hero's journey is something you can deeply relate to, something you might have experienced yourself, and - if he/she tells their story in a way that connects with you and gives you hope, you will follow them to the moon and back.

No sales pitch in the world could get you as hooked, hopeful and excited, and you will forever remember this "hero", what he went through and HOW she overcame.

Your memorable story will draw people in, first get them interested and overcome their skepticism. Again, you are appealing to people's emotions, not rational thinking.

If they connect with your story and *feel* it relates to them - even gives them goosebumps *(there is that word again...)* - they will love to hear more.

Obviously your story needs to be true, but when it is and you share it with genuine honesty and care, your audience will feel drawn to you like nothing else.

And you don't have to stop there: You can have as many stories as you want. The more the better.

Whenever you can share or explain something with a story, always choose that option.

Reaching for the Big Guns!

Connecting with the major players in your field will be a crucial fast track factor.

Just one tweet or shoutout by a major influencer can give you massive (free) exposure to hundreds of thousands - even millions of people.

Just like that!

Building those relationships takes time and you want to start during STEP 1!

You already subscribed to at least 10 major influencers in your field *(you did, right...?)*.

In addition to reading all of their material and the comment sections (or listen to/watch all their podcast and Youtube episodes), you want to start getting on their radar.

Not in a pushy, intrusive way and certainly not pitching your stuff or asking them to help or promote you - totally out of line! Don't ever do that!

Treat this like any other precious relationship you are trying to develop. Start slow and give it time, but be present continuously, so they start noticing you.

How?

1) Start by participating in the comments. Not generic, and, again, absolutely NO sharing your platform or anything about your brand.

Instead, take time and listen/watch/read carefully and leave a *thoughtful* comment. Something they might find worthwhile responding to.

Or answer questions and provide helpful information to someone else in the comments. Be sure, of course, that you are an expert in whatever you are talking about or it will have the opposite effect.

Show enthusiasm for their work. Participate on their social media. Be an active, interesting, smart commentator. Someone who adds value to the conversation. Become their greatest ambassador.

2) While going through their content, take note of aspects that could be explored further, covered in more depth. Those are the golden nuggets you can use to get in the door.

For example, if the influencer wrote an in-depth article on a particular subject, but covered one sub point with only a sentence or two, see if you can write an entire article on that sub point.

Make sure it's an important, relevant point, of course, a sub point that would add value to the influencer's audience. Again, you want to look out for *their* benefit, not yours. Make *them* look good when they share your article, so their audience will thank them and ask for more.

Whenever you can find a way to make an influencer "look good" and/or help their audience, you will get their attention. Or at least get on their radar.

Tweeting out one of your articles is easy for them. If it fits, is well written and informative, there is a good chance they will do it.

Make it a "no brainer" for them to share your content.

3) Check Buzzsumo on a regular basis and see what topics are currently trending. Is there one that this influencer has not covered that you could pitch as a guest article (more on guesting in STEP 4)? Or - if they don't accept guests, they might be willing to

share an article from your blog, thereby driving traffic to your site.

4) Find out as much as you can about that influencer. Not in a creepy, stalky way, of course, but see if there is something unique you can add. Something they would really want, even unrelated to their main topic.

Or - even better - find an area in their business where they would love to improve, but might not have the time or necessary support. Maybe you have a hack that can massively improve their situation and you offer to implement it for free.

5) A lot of influencers invite feedback in their welcome mail right after you subscribe. They invite you to tell them a little about yourself and... what your biggest struggles and frustrations are.

Can you guess why?

ALWAYS reply to those requests, because that is usually the *one* time when even a big influencer will read their fan mail and reply personally. Surprisingly, not that many subscribers respond, so a great chance for you to get noticed.

Keep your answers short, two to three paragraphs maximum. No one has time to read a long biography, this is just a first introduction. Make it count!

6) Ask them to do a written interview for your blog or next book. Keep it simple and concise. For the extra exposure, a few might be interested, and now they will know your name. To up your chances, come up with some really interesting, unusual and thoughtful questions. Not the type they get asked all the time. Impress them!

If you are interesting and stand out, they might well give you a chance even if you are brand new. Don't forget, they also started at zero and haven't forgotten those days. Most influencers are nice people and more than willing to help. They just get overloaded with selfish, whiny and unprofessional junk mail, so stand out and be patient. Your time will come.

7) Buy their products and share amazing results, aka give them a glowing testimonial. That is probably the absolute fastest way to get on any influencer's radar.

It makes *them* look good. It helps them to sell and promote their products, for example an online course, so you are adding massive benefit to their business.

Not only that: if they list your testimonial on their sales page and website, you will get a lot of additional traffic just from that. Win-win on steroids!!

In a nutshell:

The key to growing relationships with busy, successful people is to make it about *them* first and foremost.

Don't expect them to help you - certainly not for free. Don't expect them to promote you when they don't even know your name.

Grow slow, focus on ways to help *them* and their audience - not them helping *you*. In fact, that should be mostly off limits in the beginning.

I'm amazed at how often I get super long emails with extensive questions and stories from people I have never heard of. Expecting me to spend my free time to read through it all and then give detailed responses to each question.

Why would you expect that from someone you don't know? Make such a demand on their time?

Don't get me wrong, I *love* to help and I give plenty of help in my Facebook group: SassyZenGirl.Group, but to expect me to read a lengthy 10-paragraph email and then give detailed responses to each question, is inconsiderate and disrespectful of my time.

The senders are usually totally unaware and mean no harm. They are just super excited and enthusiastic and get carried away. Still though - be a professional, respect people's time and boundaries, and who they are. Time is the most precious resource and you want to be respectful of that.

Keep growing those relationships. Each will be different and require a different approach, but the above six Steps should get you started quickly and successfully.

Now let's crush it with the ultimate Instant Influencer Hack: *Bestseller Publishing*!

STEP 2:
Instant Influencer!

Bestseller Guaranteed...?!

I know, sounds crazy, but is definitely for real!

To be clear: we will not be using any shady tactics. Everything is in line with Amazon's Terms of Services, all above board. Publishing a bestseller involves understanding how Amazon's ranking algorithm works - Amazon SEO, so to speak - and how to run a "Power Launch" as I call it.

This book will *not* go over the publishing process, because that is a complex topic all on its own. Instead, I created a **special FREE 1 hour Video Training** to take you through all the steps. Over the shoulder, exactly how I research topics, plan a powerful launch and prepare my books for success, so you will be ready to go and can crush it right out of the gate!

"7 STEPS to your first #1 BESTSELLER!"

get your replay link at:
InfluencerFastTrack.com

In this chapter, we will cover 6 must-have strategies that will help you to fully *leverage* the awesome power of *Bestseller Publishing* and grow your brand (and income) to influencer status in just a few months.

Cool?

Let's rock!

Start from the End

For starters, let's remember that your books are the beginning of your influencer funnel. In fact, the most important - the FAST TRACK - factor to make everything else possible.

With that in mind, you want to structure your books in a certain way to not just sell a lot of copies, but also grow your brand and influencer status as a whole.

To do that you need a plan. You can't reach a target unless you know where you are going and while some of it will change over time, it's still important to have a roadmap in place with a clear timeline and milestones to keep you focused.

Laserlike focus.

The "where you are going" part might still seem a little fuzzy at the moment, but as you go through this book, you will gain a lot more confidence, feel empowered and get clarity about your options and how to get there.

I'm not saying it will be "easy" and it will certainly require serious commitment and effort on your part, but it *will* be a lot easier than you ever thought - and you will now have a plan and a roadmap, which makes all the difference in the world!

Then - with that roadmap in mind - craft your books as a funnel into other services or products.

You want to become clear on:

• What main service or product do you want traffic for?

• Who is the audience for that service/product?

• What book topics within your niche would be most helpful to them? What would they be <u>dying</u> to learn and read about?

• As an influencer, what other platforms do you want to employ down the road? - e.g., Podcast, Youtube Channel, Blog, Social Media, Speaking/TED, TV

• How can you tie in your branding? specific lingo/ writing style, merchandise, etc.

Defining clear answers to these questions will clarify your perspective and you are now ready to plan out the five main ingredients for publishing success:

#1: Topic Research

In the FREE Video Training I will show you how to find marketable topics on Amazon. This is crucial, because if your topic is not popular, if only a small handful of people ever search for it on Amazon, you won't get enough traffic to make this FAST TRACK blueprint work.

Don't worry about high competition. If you know how to market on Amazon, you can compete with the big boys (and gals) as you can see here (both myself and my students frequently outranking world famous authors):

#1

Negotiate without Negotiating: An Introvert's...
> Aaron Leyshon
★★★★★ 6
Kindle Edition
$0.99

#2

The Miracle Morning for Real Estate Agents: It's...
> Hal Elrod
★★★★★ 375
Kindle Edition
$9.97

> Any Department
< Kindle Store
< Kindle eBooks
Medical eBooks
Administration & Policy
Allied Health Professions
Alternative & Holistic
Basic Science
Dentistry
Diseases
Education & Training
Internal Medicine
Nursing
Pharmacology
Physician & Patient
Reference
Reproductive Medicine &
Technology

Best Sellers in Medical eBooks

Top 100 Paid   Top 100 Free

1.

Servant Leadership...
> Cara Bramlett
★★★★★ 17
Kindle Edition
$0.00

2.

The Tumor: A Non...
> John Grisham
★★★★☆ 4,156
Kindle Edition
$0.00

3. Anatomy Physiology

Anatomy and Physiology
J. Gordon Betts
★★★★★ 52
Kindle Edition
$0.00

Best Sellers in Indonesia Travel

Top 100 Paid   **Top 100 Free**

1.

BALI - Zen Traveler: A
Quick Guide f...
by G. Gabrielle
★★★★★ (16)

2.
LOOK INSIDE!

Eat Pray Love 10th-
Anniversary Editio...
by Elizabeth Gilbert
★★★★☆ (4,010)

3.

Lonely Planet Bali & Lombok
(Travel G...
by Lonely Planet
★★★☆☆ (17)

#2: Amazon SEO

SEO stands for "Search Engine Optimization" and refers to the ranking algorithm on internet platforms, including Google.

The algorithm determines who ranks in the top spots = who gets the most traffic.

When you enter a search phrase (aka "keyword") into the search bar and hit enter, you will see many different results coming up.

The ones at the top get the most attention naturally and that's where your books need to show.

No, you cannot pay for those spots, and it's not luck either. There is a method to this and it's called SEO.

In the video training I'll explain a little more, but in a nutshell: you need to "optimize" your "meta data" for "keywords" with high traffic + medium to low competition, so that your book will show in the top spots whenever anyone enters those keywords in the search bar.

Take a breath...

That was a mouthful!

Not as complicated as it sounds though: Meta data are your title, sub title, series name, book description - and even reviews. Anything on your Amazon product (book) page.

Little bots crawl every page on Amazon and read every piece of information to determine what your book is about and where they should rank you.

Other ranking factors include:

- *Social proof: number, consistent flow and average rating of your reviews*
- *Daily & 30 day average sales numbers*
- *Bounce rate = do people stay on your book page and buy or return immediately to searches*

Again - take a breath...:)

You want to find keywords (= the search phrases you put into the search bar) with good traffic and then incorporate them naturally into your title and description, so the bots will "see" them when they crawl your page and rank you for that keyword.

More on that in the video training, but keywords are a crucial factor for people to find your book - and not just during the first few weeks, but long-term.

#3/4 - Professional Cover & Title

Those two are - *by far* - the most important factors for people to buy your books. You can't be stingy here, meaning a cheap Fiverr cover does NOT cut it! You need to look professional and convey the style of your brand.

You also need to spend some time crafting a marketable, catchy title with sub title incorporating a few keywords (more on that in the video). Crafting well converting titles and headlines is an art form and you will need some training to make it pop.

PRO TIP: Never get attached to a title (or cover) or try to be too clever or cute. Usually people won't 'get it' and they won't spend the time to figure it out. They will simply move on. You have 2-3 seconds to capture their attention. So, catchy, yes, but clear, simple, to the point. No guess work needed.

There is a science to well converting title templates, the ones that trigger us to buy. It's called "Copywriting" and the top guns in this field make millions. Why? Because the subtle difference of just a few words can so drastically increase sales numbers and thereby revenue, that companies will pay extraordinary sums for good copy.

If this is new to you, please take the time to learn it and run your titles by someone with a lot experience - and listen to their advice. It can literally make the difference between zero and thousands of dollars in sales.

If you want to test your copywriting chops, you can find a little quiz on the **Resources page**.

#5 - A Power Launch

How? - you might wonder if you don't have any followers yet?

Fortunately, there are a number of great Kindle promo services that will present your book to their large audiences (often hundreds of thousands of avid readers) for a nominal fee. Anywhere between $5-120.

All you have to do is, book 2-3 every day for 7 days and your book will start selling - no question!

As the promos start selling your book you will rise in the bestseller ranks in just a few days - and it doesn't take that many sales to reach the Top 100 in a sub category. According to Amazon, being among the Top 100 books in any category counts as a bestseller.

Crucial here is your topic. The greatest marketing strategy can't sell your book if people aren't interested or if your book looks unprofessional (cheap, self-made cover, amateurish title, etc.).

On the other hand, a highly popular topic will usually sell like hot cakes with the help of these promos. Again, you can't be stingy, only run two $5 promos and expect to rank #1. It takes continuously increasing sales over at least 7 days to "trigger" - there is that magic word - the algorithm, so Amazon will keep promoting the book FOR you!

How awesome is *that*?!

There are more strategies for long term sales, of course, but for now that should have gotten your juices going!

You can DO this!

Really!

And nothing will compare to the speed and efficiency of *Bestseller Publishing* to grow any platform or business while Amazon actually *pays* you (aka royalties) to grow your brand, get more subscribers and become an influencer!

Take another breath....:)

Once again, for a detailed, over the shoulder look at the publishing process, be sure to check out the **video training at InfluencerFastTrack.com.**

Draw 'em in!

"The Sassy Way to.......when you have NO CLUE!"

With a pink, cartoonish cover.

Not your everyday blogging or Wordpress guide, but it sold well from the start and stands out among all other books in its genre *(for better or worse...)*.

Not everyone will want a pink "NO CLUE" book and that's perfectly fine.

They wouldn't be the right audience and by positioning myself in this unique way, I'm attracting a specific reader personality.

Not so much specific demographics I found - they are all over the place for this book - but definitely a certain personality type with a good sense of humor facing similar challenges, like struggling with tech and/or marketing.

Fun, friendly, excited and with a spunk.

If you've been in our Facebook group, you know what I mean (SassyZenGirl.Group).

Tone and writing style also match cover and title.

A fun, laid back blogging style that is easy to read, easy to understand - and not dreary and boring.

In other words, a writing style that matches the pink/ NO CLUE brand.

Speaking of **Writing Style**:

To connect with your readers, you want to keep it fun and engaging. More a conversation than a lecture.

Like a good friend helping the reader solve a problem in a fun, entertaining way.

Short sentences, frequent paragraphs, humor.

Talk WITH them like a good friend, not AT them.

One of the great weaknesses I see with a lot of self-published books is a lack of good writing.

If you are not experienced, no problem: find good training and *definitely* hire an experienced copy/content editor, not just a proofreader.

You can't afford to look amateurish and unless you are an experienced writer with years of practice, you are not a qualified judge of your own writing. Sorry to be blunt, but I mean well.

It is all perception and you need to look professional. Good writing, free of grammar and spelling errors is key (I made the mistake early on not to hire a proofreader - many first time authors do - and I came to regret it very quickly!).

Henneke Duistermaat shares some great (free) "snackable" writing tips and Jon Morrow is one of the best in the business. His blog *Smartblogger* shares an abundance of tips on writing and engaging an audience. Both are great free resources and will point you in the right direction.

On the **Resources Page** you can find one of Jon's most famous posts, shared over a million times and with an amazing story that will give you goosebumps.

If you want to take it one step further, Jon's Guest Blogging Course is one of the best investments I have ever made and was largely responsible for my quick success as an author. The course does not just cover how to land prestigious guest spots and find trending topics, but most of all, how to *write* well! How to structure your writing, craft winning titles and draw readers in with the first line and opening paragraph: the famous "Morrow Opening". You can try it out for 30 Days and the link on the **Resources Page** will give you a 30% Discount.

Write the best book on your Topic

This may seem obvious, but when you are using your books to funnel traffic to your other ventures, you might be tempted to leave out important steps, so readers have to buy your courses and services to actually implement what you teach.

Bad idea - and a missed opportunity!

Why?

Because:

1) Amazon readers are very savvy and critical. If they sense that your book is nothing but a sales pitch, you will hear about it in the reviews!

And they won't be subtle about it.

2) You are trying to grow a loyal following and why would people follow you if you treat them that way? It's disrespectful. Doesn't mean you have to share every single detail, nor is that even possible with the limited constraints of a book, but even those who are not buying anything else from you should find great value and a compact road map to success.

3) Overdeliver and write the absolute best book on your topic. Help as much as you can. This way, readers will be:

- impressed by your expertise
- grateful at how much you helped them
- grateful that you are so generous with a low priced book
- believe - and this is crucial for selling high ticket items - that if your book is already so awesome, how amazing must your services and courses be!

- want to be coached by you personally and consider it an honor
- become ardent, loyal fans
- buy every book you write
- get pre-qualified with that first sale => tripwire (see funnel magic in Part 1)

Instead of giving a little teaser, leaving readers frustrated.

4) View your books as the most amazing opportunity you could ever have to show new readers, clients and customers what amazing help you have to offer.

Without being pitchy, salesy or annoying and without having to pester people or give away free "test" sessions.

Instead, with awesome, mind-blowing information, tips and methods to greatly improve their lives, whatever it is they need.

Be a friend who is genuinely interested to help and not just trying to sell more books and other products.

Build a relationship of trust and respect.

How to (non) pitch your Stuff

How then *do* you mention your business and services without being pitchy, salesy and annoying?

That's actually pretty easy to do:

Naturally include your other business ventures and activities as they relate to your book. Rather than giving a sales pitch at the end for your coaching or courses, use LOTs of examples and case studies from your practice where it fits naturally (not pitchy). Make it mouth watering and amazing, so people will be *dying* to achieve the same results and want to work with you.

One of the most obvious choices to funnel your book traffic into are services related to your topic. This could be:

- *Coaching*
- *Consulting*
- *Professional Services (lawyer, CPA, health care, etc.)*
- *Freelancing*
- *Done-for-You Services*

If you already have an active practice and are looking to grow your client base, a how-to guide on a hot topic in your niche is a great way to start.

I would keep the first book simple, not too long, not necessarily the big, major masterpiece that you will be known for.

Ideally, pick something you know really well and can write down in a week - like I did with the blogging book.

That way, you can focus most of your time on the publishing part (which will be a little overwhelming the first time) without being bogged down by a difficult, lengthy book to write.

A "practice" book so to speak, but one that should still be popular and sell well. If you make a few mistakes (and who doesn't the first time?) it won't be such a drama, plus you can move on quickly to the next.

Getting that first book out and to bestseller status will change *everything* for you. After that milestone, everything will become a lot easier and you will have gained valuable insight that you can apply in your next book.

If you want to go with a major book even the first time around - by all means, go for it!

No need to wait or tone things down. But if you are still deciding on your main topic and are a little scared of the whole process, a practice book is not a bad idea.

Back to your (non) pitching:

As we mentioned several times now, be sure to first conduct some in-depth research to find out what clients most urgently need help with. Don't guess or pick what you would *like* to write about. Instead, find your clients' biggest frustrations, pain points or needs - and then provide the *best* possible solution.

Here are some more pointers to turn your books into irresistible "client magnets":

#1 - Each book needs to be absolutely awesome and *really* help readers achieve amazing results. No cookie-cutter mumbo jumbo that can be found everywhere else. Yours needs to stand out and share techniques and methods that can't be found anywhere else. Readers must be blown away and enthusiastic after reading your book.

Remember, your book can become your greatest PR motor and sales pitch, without ever sounding like one. If you are looking for clients, your book is your job interview. If you are selling a product, it replaces your sales page.

That's how powerful this is!

#2 - Share case studies from your practice throughout your book. The more amazing, the better. Nothing will make readers want to hire you more than success stories. If you don't have any yet, give out some free sessions, *really* help people and then ask for testimonials. I don't usually recommend free sessions except for a quick 15 min. intro, because they invite freeloaders and devalue your service. However, testimonials & success stories are so crucially important, that I would consider them the *one* rare exception in the beginning.

#3 - This should be obvious, but... make sure people know how to contact you. No need to be pitchy or salesy, just mention your services in the conclusion and again on a separate page after the final chapter. Both showing a way to get in touch with you (website, email address, etc.).

For coaching or consulting you shouldn't start for less than $97 per hour. Even as a beginner!

As a bestselling author with readers all around the world (yes, on Amazon your audience will be worldwide!) you can actually charge quite a bit more.

People will view you differently, especially if they loved your book: They will admire you. They will understand that your time is precious, and if you undersell, you will lose their respect. This is another reason why you should never give out free sessions, except a brief 15 minute "interview" or for testimonial purposes.

A smart pricing hack - especially if you feel a little insecure in the beginning - would be to offer an "introductory rate" or a "special discount for your readers" for the first session (or 3-pak of sessions).

Your official price per session could be $197 and you are offering a "limited time" 50% discount as an "introductory rate" or a "special rate for your readers".

Suddenly, $97 doesn't sound so much anymore. In fact, in the perception of your readers, $97 is now a really great deal, especially when you add a time limit to create urgency and make it exclusive to your readers. VIP treatment!

See how easy marketing can be?

And that's just one of many hacks.

Here is another one:
Rather than just offering your services (especially, coaching and consulting), let people know how they can "apply" to be "considered" for your services. That puts *you* in the driver seat: you are the decision maker and not desperate to be hired. It totally changes the dynamic, because readers now realize it is a *privilege* to get your services and *you* choose who you work with.

As a bestselling author, readers will assume that you get many requests and can pick and choose. Even if that isn't the case in the beginning, letting potential clients "apply" and see if you will "accept" them, makes you a lot more attractive and will make for a much better client-coach relationship than if people can just hire you whenever they want.

Keypoints in a nutshell:
#1 - Research and be *sure* your service is urgently needed. The more niched down the better. We all love

specialists and are willing to pay a lot more for specialty services.

#2 - Have a unique method that brings *amazing* results. Ideally quickly, so people will want more and are ready to book prepaid packages, rather than just a single session. Possibly even a long-term monthly retainer.

#3 - If needed, do a few free sessions to get testimonials and amazing case studies, but *only* for that purpose. If your book is awesome, you don't need to prove yourself again with a free "test" session. Instead, readers are lucky to book you.

Whether you are new or already have an active practice, write your book with the above in mind. Make it a no-brainer that people will want to hire you after reading your book. Meaning, give *amazing* information that will help readers right away. Share case studies that will have readers dying to work with you to achieve similar results.

Give a lot of actionable advice. You might even include an "Action Tip" at the end of each chapter and add a cheat sheet or checklist as your freebie offer. Frequently remind people to take action and not just read your book. Invite them to share their results in your Facebook group and ask questions.

Stories will add the magic touch that will keep readers glued. There is nothing more seductive - and educational - than a story or a real life example. It makes the reading experience fun and easy.
For our purposes, they also serve as the best marketing tool you could have - without ever seeming that way.

Done-for-you Services

Done-for-you services have become immensely popular in recent years. Everyone is busy and especially if your topic involves tech or marketing skills, people are usually relieved if they can pay someone to do it *for* them, even if they just read your entire book on the topic!
In fact, they will come with a much greater appreciation, now that they know all that's involved!

The Evergreen Bestseller Hack

What the bootie is that?!

Well, quite simply, a series of shorter books around the same main topic. Each book highlighting a different aspect.

Why?

Because with a series, all books help sell each other. You can cross-promote, and there is something irresistible, almost addictive, about owning the entire series.

Readers tell me all the time how they bought all the books in the *SassyZenGirl* series. They even mention it in the reviews quite often! A series is a powerful brand builder and allows readers, (i.e., potential clients and customers) to get to know you and start identifying with your brand, wanting to be a part of it.

By series I mean have Amazon set it up (you can't do it yourself) so all the thumbnails show underneath each book:

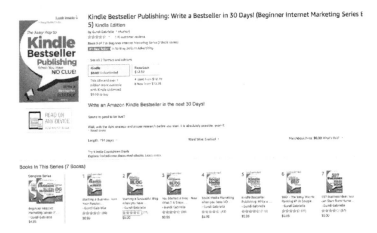

These are free little mini ads and make it incredibly easy for people to buy all your books - and you *always* want to make it as easy as possible!

And guess what? "Customers also bought" also featuring pink domination...

Take that for growing brand awareness!

So, once you've narrowed down your sub niche and the overall topic you want to write about, start planning a series that ties in with your business and can serve as a powerful funnel opener for your entire brand.

Not everyone will become a long-term customer, and they don't need to be, but you are building a core of loyal clients that will become passionate ambassadors for your brand and recommend you to everyone they know.

Subscribers on Autopilot

Once you have your series in place, be sure to include a lead magnet, also called a "freebie offer", that readers will get access to in exchange for their email address.

Popular freebies are:

- *FREE report*
- *Cheat sheet*
- *Checklist*
- *Action guide*
- *Resources list*

all related to your topic for massive, automatic list building. More on list building in STEP 3, but this part is relevant to your books:

How do you find a well-converting lead magnet?

Here is a simple hack:

Rather than guessing and hoping for the best, find out what already works and model it. Here is how:

Look through the top bestselling indie books in your field and see what lead magnets they are using. The "Look Inside" feature makes this really easy as they usually come right after the Table of Contents. If the book has been out for at least three months, you can be pretty sure that their lead magnet is converting well, or they would have changed it by now.

Obviously, do not copy! Instead, model the *type* of lead magnet they are using and give it your own spin.

Or go through the top blogs in your niche and check out their lead magnets (usually found in the side bar or on a hyperactive pop-up). You can even contact the blog owner and ask them what templates have worked well for them.

No need to reinvent the wheel and try for months on end. Better spend your time writing more books and growing your business.

Once you have created your lead magnet, add it as a bonus offer in the beginning, middle, and/or end of your book.

When readers click on the link, they are taken to a landing page like this:

Grab your

FREE Domain
Name Report

Gimme!

where they can submit their email address and then collect the freebie via a link in their inbox.

You need a simple landing page template like the above and a mailing list provider like Mailchimp or AWeber to store email addresses and send out messages. *Thrive Architect* offers a large selection of premade templates where you can simply change text, color, and images, and have an awesome looking landing page in no time.

More Income on Autopilot

Bestseller traffic can easily be funneled into affiliate products related to your niche for a nice passive side income right from the start.

What is affiliate marketing?

Simply put, a referral fee for products you recommend.

You get a product link that includes your unique affiliate ID for tracking purposes.

When someone buys that product using your link, you earn an affiliate commission.

On autopilot!

Affiliate marketing is one of the easiest and most effective ways to earn passive income online and can easily be included in your books.

IMPORTANT: While Amazon, too, has a big affiliate program for all their products, including books, you are *__not__ allowed to use Amazon affiliate links in Kindle books!*

Outside affiliate programs are fine and can include softwares, online courses, or other products related to what you teach.

How to find suitable products?

#1 - Start by looking at all the products you are already using. Find out if they have an affiliate program (usually listed in the footer of the company website or simply google the **[company name] + "affiliate"**).

#2 - Google **[your niche]** + "affiliate" and see if you find anything useful. Also, "**Top 10 affiliate programs for [your niche]**" or "**Best affiliate programs for [your niche]**".

#3 - FASTEST METHOD: Check the **Tools** or **Resources** section of the top blogs in your niche. They will be full of affiliate products because affiliate marketing is one of the most effective and lucrative monetization methods for blogs.

You can also use the blog's search function and enter **Review**. Review posts are a classic way to market affiliate products and should bring up the most lucrative products this blogger promotes.

Using option #3 ensures that you only work with legitimate companies that will pay you honestly and on time. Plus, these are products that readers obviously like, so you follow what works instead of reinventing the wheel.

Once you find a few products that fit well with your topic and assist in what you teach, sign up as an affiliate and start using their affiliate link when mentioning the product in your book.

That's it. Quite simple, really, and easy income on autopilot as long as:

• you only recommend <u>amazing</u> products that you use yourself and stand fully behind.

• your products are <u>crucial</u> to whatever you teach and make life a lot easier (not a luxury, but a necessity).

• you don't overdo it. Only use a few where it makes sense. Otherwise, readers will leave angry comments in the reviews.

From now on, always be on the lookout for affiliate programs whenever you do a course or start using a new software or product. Most will have affiliate programs, and you can start by mentioning them on your website's Resources section or by writing a review post.

Now, let's grow your tribe!

STEP 3:
Inspire Your Tribe!

Alrighty!

You've published your first bestseller and have new subscribers and social media followers coming in on autopilot.

Now is the time to convert those one-time readers into long-term fans.

Exciting times!

If readers loved your book, you are already halfway there. They obviously respect you and your expertise and gel with your style. You got past the "first date." Now you can grow that date into a long-term relationship.

You have three channels to connect with your readers, each serving a different purpose:

• Your mailing list
• Your social media
• Your Facebook group

If you feel overwhelmed, start with email and a Facebook group and add other social media later.

Why?

Because a Facebook group allows you to connect with your audience in a fun, relaxed, and most of all, unintrusive way, unlike email where readers quickly grow annoyed if you mail too often or never open it.

What's more, a group allows your fans to interact with each other, become friends, and turn into a close-knit community where people know each other.

Your community (or "tribe" as is the hip name these days) is where the magic happens. Build a strong, passionate community, and your brand will be on stable ground for a long time to come.

Forums used to be the go-to place for community building, but everyone is so busy these days that even the extra step of joining a forum, filling out a profile, and logging in every time will prevent many from participating.

On the other hand, almost everyone is on Facebook, usually on a daily basis, so clicking a button _one_ time to join a group and then seeing all group posts in the timeline is the path of least resistance and highly effective to grow your tribe quickly. Plus, profiles are already filled out, nothing else to do. Easy! And you _want_ to make things as easy as possible with the least amount of steps.

As for email, mailing lists are a must. Your mailing list will be your most valuable marketing asset, because you own it and have complete control over it.

Social media and Amazon can change their rules at any time, and they often do! They could even shut you down or block your account for a while.

You need one market "asset" that you fully control, and your mailing list will be just that.

What about Social Media?

What I'm sharing here is different from mainstream marketing advice. Then again, mainstream doesn't usually have a series of bestselling books to get traffic from. Most have to take the arduous route of chasing followers one by one.

Very time consuming. Very tedious.

As a best-selling author, readers will automatically want to follow you on social media because they want to hear about updates and what else you are up to.

As I mentioned in STEP 2, your books are your business card and sales pitch. Except, it doesn't feel like a pitch.

This is your moment to shine and share all the ways you can help people, and what makes you different.

It is also your opportunity to *connect* with your audience which is why you want to write in a fun, conversational style. Definitely write the book yourself and don't leave it to a ghostwriter.

With that connection in place, you don't have to beg people to follow you. Many will naturally be interested, and you can focus on cultivating those who have joined rather than spending tedious time getting followers.

If you only have time for email and your Facebook group, that's OK. You can always invite your followers to join you on other platforms later. If they love your brand they will gladly do so, no need to stress on it for now.

You should still have a Facebook Business/Fan Page because you need one to run Facebook ads. Plus, a Facebook Page is standard for any legitimate business these days, so for appearances' sake, you should set one up.

It is important to understand though that unlike with Facebook groups, your fan page followers will not automatically see your posts in their timeline.

Yep, that's right. Page owners compete with each other for a spot in the timeline of *each* follower, and only very few get through. Only 6 percent of your followers might actually see any of your posts in their timeline!

The bigger, more authoritative - and *active* - a page is (comments, likes, shares), the better the chances of winning the competition. The time of day also plays a part. There is such a thing as "rush hour" on Facebook, meaning lots of pages posting at the same time, resulting in more competition versus other times when it's easier to get through.

The decision who gets featured is automated through Facebook's algorithm, and unless you post often and have a lot of engagement from your followers, it will be very difficult to get featured.

A workaround are Facebook ads. You can boost your posts and select your followers as target audience. That's easy to do, and $5 will already make a difference. The video on the **Resources Page** will show you how to set them up should you need help.

While timeline competition is unique to Facebook, *all* social media are crowded and competitive, and your time might be better spent elsewhere in the beginning.

It also depends on your niche. As a travel blogger, you absolutely need to start growing your Instagram following from day one. That is the gold standard for travel influencers. Potential sponsors and partners will usually first check your Instagram following and are *actively searching Instagram* to find new travel influencers to partner with.

Your niche might have a different emphasis, and you can always tell by following major influencers to see which platform you should focus on.

The point is: you can't do everything. Not if you want to keep quality high. So you want to pick whatever is *most* important to growing your brand (and income) <u>at this very moment</u>, and then focus fully on that.

One or two things at a time, three maximum, or nothing will get done properly.

That's why I recommend starting with your mailing list and a Facebook group. Learn the ropes, get a system in place, and then hire a virtual assistant to do the leg work for you, including as community manager in your group.

You might even find someone among the group members who would be a perfect fit and would love to fill that role.

Virtual Staff Finder can be another option for finding a Virtual Assistant: **SassyZenGirl.com/VA**

Tim Ferriss famously started the VA movement in the *Four Hour Work Week*, one of the best business books of all time, and STEP 3 could be a good time for you to start if you haven't already.

By the way, VAs are not just secretaries, though they can fulfill that role as well. You can get help from SEO VAs, social media VAs, content writer VAs, customer service VAs, graphic design Vas, and many more.

You still need to remain active and present in your group and certainly with your emails, but you don't have to run everything, find content to share, take care of admin areas, customer support, etc.

If you do have the time, add one more social media platform, but make sure you find good training and learn all the hacks to grow quickly. This will be different for each platform, and YouTube has a wealth of great (free) information as do *Social Media Examiner* and similar sites.

Overall, from my experience I would say that social media platforms are not the most effective avenue when you first try to grow your brand if - you use *Bestseller Publishing* as your main traffic source.
One thing at a time and down the road, definitely add more platforms, but you don't have to stress and overwhelm yourself right from the start.

<u>In a nutshell:</u>

Growing a strong, vibrant community is the foundation of influencer status. That is what influence stands for, and that is why companies are willing to shelve out thousands of dollars for sponsorships because a well-connected influencer can massively grow their sales numbers with just one tweet, social media post, or email.

Therefore, focus on community building first and foremost without stretching too thin. The easiest and most effective strategy will be your very own Facebook group or the intimate one-on-one communication of email. More on that in a moment.

First, though:

Make it fun!

How then do you grow a passionate tribe?

Here are some GOODIES to help you rock it:

#1 - ENGAGE

Ask their opinion
Make it fun and exciting to be a part of your brand. An easy way to engage people is by simply asking their opinion. Use a poll, for example.

In my Facebook group, members frequently share their cover or title options and let the group vote. Those are always the most popular posts! People love them and often give interesting feedback.

Outside of Facebook, you can use a free plugin like WP Poll on your blog or a free software like Wufoo (also for surveys).

Feedback will be more immediate and fun in a Facebook group because members can see each other's votes and can interact, but for a more in-depth survey, a separate page might be better suited.

Set a challenge
As an example: you could make it a regular practice on Mondays to ask everyone to list their goals for the week, and then follow up on Friday or Sunday to let people share their results.

Or you start a 30-day challenge in a separate post, so members can update their progress in the comments and see how others are doing.

You can even run a little competition with a prize for the winner at the end. Great motivation and fun!

AMAs and Facebook Live
AMA stands for "Ask Me Anything" and has become the cyber cool for Q&A with your followers. Facebook Live is one way to do it—all live *(obviously!)* —or you collect questions in a comment thread and then create a video with your answers. Easy to do and fun for your followers.

Quiz
Quizzes are fun, get great engagement, and often go viral. Best of all, you can require that participants

provide their email address to get access to the results. Meaning, when your group members share the quiz with their friends, you will get new subscribers and possibly group members with very little effort. *Thrive Themes* offers a great, easy-to-use quiz builder.

#2 - VIP TREATMENT

Exclusive offers

Reward your members with special offers they cannot get anywhere else. Examples:

- *special discounts once in a while*
- *a free day for your books*
- *a special training webinar only for members*
- *advance notice and pricing for new products*

Whatever applies to your business, try to compile a list of things you can offer every once in a while to show your followers how much you appreciate them and how awesome it is to follow you.

For inspiration, join some of the top groups in your field, see what big influencers offer, and what their followers particularly like. You'll quickly get a sense of what works and can then develop your own unique style.

#3 - EDUCATE AND SUPPORT

While it is perfectly fine to occasionally pitch a product or affiliate offer, the majority of your posts and emails should be pure value.

Offer great information, helpful articles, support to people's questions, cheat sheets, templates, videos. Whatever is most helpful to your peeps, create a schedule and add awesome stuff on a regular basis.

When you treat your followers with that kind of respect, they will often actually *ask* for your affiliate link when buying a new product because they appreciate your help and want to return the favor. They know you are getting a commission and they *want* you to get that commission! Isn't that a much nicer way of doing business than badgering people and hammering for every sale?

#4 - NAME YOUR TRIBE

You might have noticed how major influencers often have a special name for their fans. Something like:

"[brand name] Nation", "[brand name] Universe", "[brand name] Tribe"
or a branded name like:

"Sumolings" (from AppSumo)

That way people identify with your brand in a very personal way. They feel that they are a part of something awesome, a cool movement, and that is quite irresistible.

Merchandise is another great way to grow your movement. More on that later.

For now, let's take a closer look at your mailing list and Facebook group, and how you can make the most of each:

The Mucho Bling Asset!

Also called a mailing List.

What do I mean?

We already talked about the importance of cultivating an active mailing list and you will see in the later STEPS how amazingly powerful your list can become to massively grow your business and income.

Absolutely phenomenal!

How then can you grow that list and more importantly, keep people active and responsive, keeping in mind how overloaded and crowded most inboxes are?

Every niche and audience will be different, but in general, emailing two to three times per month or once per week is about as much as most audiences will tolerate before unsubscribe rates will spike.

Some leading marketers recommend mailing every day or even more than that, so that people won't "forget" you. One famous sales guru even advised:

"If you aren't getting a 20 percent refund rate, you're not selling aggressively enough."

You can replace "refund" with "unsubscribe" as that quote is often referenced by aggressive email marketers.

This might have worked a few years ago and maybe it still does for a few niches, especially on recreational topics. Fiction readers often *love* to hear about their favorite character and actually enjoy daily mails and updates. For anything related to business or nonfiction, though, it is usually not a good idea and can cause a lot of unsubscribes from people who might have otherwise stayed.

I have certainly unsubscribed a few times when I actually really liked the sender but couldn't take the constant bombardment anymore. And I was a paying customer...

You have probably, too.

As for "so people won't forget you," that is a sad statement. If you have a *unique* brand, really help people and built relationships with your tribe, they won't forget you. Quite the opposite!

Major influencers like Pat Flynn, Gary V. or Josh Steimle do send emails regularly, but I couldn't even tell you the frequency, because it doesn't feel that often (certainly not daily or every 2-3 days). I'm happy being subscribed to them.

You can also run a survey with your audience to see how *they* feel about frequency. Your subscribers will appreciate the courtesy and be more tolerant in the future, and you can fine-tune your email marketing.

Also, keep in mind: subscribers who come through your books already feel like they know you. They are warm to hot leads, meaning people who are interested in you and *want* to hear more, unlike cold leads from Facebook ads or Google traffic.

You don't want to ruin that goodwill by going overkill with emails.

It's fine to occasionally pitch something as long as it's high quality and useful, but communication should be so amazing that readers quickly realize that they are missing out if they don't read your mails.

*A **QUICK HACK** to get attention:*

Give a digital product away for free to the first 10 responders. As an example, I recently offered a new (smaller) course for free to the first 10 responders, followed by another 20 at a 90% discount. As you might expect, the 10 free spots were filled within minutes, and the remaining 90% spots soon after. Many who didn't make it wrote follow up mails telling me how much they would have loved to win and thanking me for the offer.

In some cases, this was the first time I had ever heard from them!

More exciting:

The open rate of the next mail following this freebie offer was a whopping 76%!

Obviously, you can't do giveaways all the time, nor do you want to train your audience to wait for freebies, but do something exciting every once in a while — something that gets them engaged. Examples could be:

- Ask them what topics they would like you to cover.
- Have them vote on their TOP 10 favorite posts on your blog.
- Ask their favorite authors or books in your field and why (or podcasters, bloggers, YouTubers, etc.).
- Share an a-ha moment they had through your teaching or how it inspired action. You could even make it a competition with the winners getting featured in an upcoming post, or even cooler, your next book! Subject line: *"I want to feature you in my next book!"*
- Run a quiz. Great viral potential. (Thrive, once again, has a great quiz builder.)
- Run a larger survey and share the results in an extensive blog post with quotes from your audience with their permission.
- Let them vote on a new mascot or name.
- Share a pivotal life story and how it changed you. Ask them to share their own, either publicly or just with you. This can also be featured in a series of blog posts.

The list goes on, but this hopefully gives you some ideas.

It's also nice to share what you are up to right now, what's happening in your life, some personal story.

Makes for a better hook and opening and people will often reply and share a story of their own.

In other words, start the conversation. Share like you would with a good friend. Let them take part in your life, at least a little.

For the autoresponder (the automated follow-up sequence for new subscribers during their first few weeks), you can continue what you teach in the books.

Focus on one aspect at a time. Go more in-depth, maybe share a video or remind them of important aspects. You can also include an affiliate product where it fits naturally. A software that's helpful for that particular step or a book or course.

Also invite feedback.

The first or second email could include an invite to the new subscriber to tell you a little more about themselves and answer one to two questions. For example: their favorite_____ (related to your topic).

Plus, the all-important:

What is your biggest frustration with [your topic]?

What do you struggle with the most?

Those are great to get a conversation started, get to know your readers, and fine-tune your content!

Remember reverse engineering?

The better you know what your followers need, the better you can help them, and the more loyal and grateful they will be.

These are just a few initial pointers.

I find that one of the best ways to learn great email copy is to subscribe to those who do it really well. Ideally, in a style and tone very similar to yours. It doesn't even have to be in your niche.

Whenever you come across a website or blog that you resonate with, in particular, the writing style and how they communicate with you, the reader, subscribe to their list and check out their email copy and autoresponder.

Also keep a list of great subject lines, the ones that really get you to open.

Model what works is a theme throughout this book and makes it surprisingly easy and fun to learn the best strategies. Be it finding a good lead magnet, writing email copy, landing pages, and even book titles.

This is just for starters, of course, to help you in the beginning when so much is new, and there's so much to learn. Once you find your groove, you will develop your own language and tone, but if that seems difficult at first:

Model what works.

The Chill Factor...

Let's get chillin' with your peeps!

How to grow your Facebook group into a vibrant, fun community?

Here is the key:

Most Facebook groups are sloppily run—more of a vanity project by the owner than an active, friendly community that support each other.

You need to set the tone from the start and be your very best example. Invite members to support each other, cheer on success stories, ask and give feedback, and welcome everyone personally.

Encourage this spirit from day 1 and you will be amazed at what can happen.

It took me a long time to realize how amazing Facebook can be and that it doesn't take a lot of time to run them effectively. That's really what had kept me from doing it for a long time. Boy, was I wrong, and thank Goodie, I finally started one only a few months ago.

You can join here, by the way:

SassyZenGirl.Group

I remember in the beginning, we only had a small handful of people. On the second day one member shared how she had landed an amazing guest post. No one responded or even hit the Like button. I started a new post inviting everyone to congratulate her and share in her joy - and to help create a warm, friendly environment that helps everyone grow.

That was all they needed! They jumped right in, cheered her on, and we've never looked back. They just didn't know.

They were new and didn't know what to expect. Most Facebook groups are pretty anonymous, people only posting when they need something, but otherwise, not really paying attention.

In our group, most members actively participate daily or at least a few times a week. For many, it's their first stop of the day even if they don't need anything.

There is always something interesting going on - someone publishing another book, working on a project, or sharing a tip. People know each other by name and frequently converse in the comments.

It's a fun place to be and many members have remarked how different this group is and how it is the only group they actively participate in. Plus, they get a lot of advice and support and every venture is more easy and fun when you don't have to go it alone.

I greet everyone personally, once a day in a group post, and as you can see, they are getting a warm and enthusiastic welcome:

I invite new members to introduce themselves and share what they are working on or might need help with and other group members comment and show an interest under their post. Everyone feels welcome and supported from the day they come in.

I also make it clear that while we love to help, it needs to be a two-way street.

In most groups, members only post when they want something, but never give back or show any interest in others. Not so here.

Nor any kind of pitching, scamming, rudeness, or off-topic comments, which haven't been much of a problem, but would not be tolerated.

It's not about the numbers...

With both mailing lists and groups, I find that quality is much more important than quantity. I'm not too interested in growing the biggest group possible, but rather focus on quality and giving each member help and attention as well as a chance to meet and know each other. That's how you grow an active, passionate community.

Chris M. Walker aka "Superstar SEO" *(really!)*, one of the best SEOs on the planet, grew his Facebook group last year from a few hundred to 12,000 *(yep, that's right)* and was featured on Ahrefs (= top SEO platform) as one of the top 15 Facebook groups SEOs should join! He is now close to 20,000 members at the time of this writing.

Chris built a friendly, supportive, and very engaged community where he provides awesome content and offers amazing special deals from his SEO business just for group members. Initially, he ran his business out of Konker, an SEO gig platform similar to Fiverr, and was able to turn that business into multiple six figures as the top seller on the entire platform.

Not enough with that. He then leveraged the amazing following he had grown in his Facebook group and launched his own gig platform *Legiit*, all with the backing and enthusiastic support of his then-12,000+ loyal members.

Chris credits his rapid success largely to the power of his Facebook group and the ease it provided him to reach and interact with his customers.

His example inspired me to start the *SassyZenGirl Networking Group*, and it's been absolutely amazing.

For both me and the readers.

It has turbocharged my book and course sales. I gain amazing insights into more ways to help people and provide valuable, marketable content. It's fun and rewarding to get to know your readers on such a personal level, and it created a supportive community under the *SassyZenGirl* brand!

The support of this group has already helped many newbie authors, bloggers, and entrepreneurs in their launches.

Members passionately love this group as you can see:

 . Welcome everyone. I have to say that I'm part of a bunch of groups - but this one is the BEST by far because it's so active and collaborative. Gundi's participation is what makes it so worthwhile. She cares about the members and is extremely active here.

Branding Bonanza!

Once you have built an enthusiastic following and a warm, friendly community, people will start to identify with your brand and want to share their enthusiasm publicly. That's when merchandise and other unique, fun products can make it ever more cool and fun to be a part of your brand:

Merchandise

Whether it be T-shirts, baseball caps, bags, pens, mouse pads or... super cute - a stuffed animal of your mascot, merchandise is a powerful way to spread your brand and make it fun for your fans to be a part of.

Journals, Greeting Cards, Calendars

Your brand might lend itself to journals, workbooks, greeting cards, or calendars. All can help you grow your brand and create a nice passive income stream while providing an additional resource to your followers.

John Lee Dumas from the #1 ranked podcast *Entrepreneur on Fire* created *The Mastery Journal* and *The Freedom Journal* to help his followers reach their goals. These are beautifully bound hard cover books, and he financed production with one of the most successful crowdfunding campaigns in history. In fact, in the article on the **Resources Page** he shares some awesome tips on how to really rock it:

How to CRUSH Kickstarter: $453K in 33 days and the 6th most funded publishing campaign of all time

You can also spread your brand virtually with **branded social media cards**. Get a nice design with your website and hashtag at the bottom and share quotes from your books, either your own or someone famous.

Quote cards can easily go viral, so it's worth hiring a designer to maximize effectiveness. *Fiverr* has many good $5 gigs. Or you can use templates in *Canva* and create them yourself. Canva is a free software with many beautiful, predesigned templates. You simply drag and drop, change colors, fonts, and images, and have a professionally looking social card in no time.

Here are three more options to keep things interesting and fun for your fans:

Physical Products and e-commerce

If applicable you could create physical products related to your topic or start a niche related e-commerce store that complements your service.

Richie Norton's company *Prouduct* who also facilitated manufacturing and production of JLD's *Freedom* and *Mastery Journals* can produce pretty much any product you can envision. They work with suppliers and manufacturers in China and other countries, keeping things cost effective while overseeing the entire process from beginning to finish.

Multimedia

Another option are multimedia products related to your field like meditation CDs or workout DVDs to name just a few.

Once again, you can use a print-on-demand (POD) option to keep things simple. *CD Baby* produces and distributes CDs. *Createspace* produces both CDs and DVDs with distribution via Amazon.

Apps

An app for your brand - how cool is *that*?

Whatever your field, there is usually an area where an app could be useful and all you have to do is hire a developer to create one.

It's by far not as complex and expensive as a full-fledged software and yet another avenue to stay in touch with your followers. Most of them are glued to their phones anyway, and you become ever more present in their lives in a good, helpful way. Great for branding also.

Not all of the above will be relevant to your niche, but pick one or two and add them to your portfolio over time.

Your audience will love the new adventure, and you can create a few more passive income streams.

STEP 4:
Be Everywhere!

Let's spread your awesomeness!

Now that you have laid the groundwork and your following is growing, it is time to expand your exposure. You want to show up everywhere so people start noticing you and begin to perceive you as a regular presence.

One of the most powerful methods to achieve that is guesting on big blogs and podcasts.

As one of the classic OPA methods, guesting allows you to leverage peer and influencer audiences, both short and long-term.

The biggest exposure comes when your guest article or podcast first goes live, but it doesn't end there. For years to come, people will see your article or episode on that influencer's website (or iTunes listing), sending you an evergreen stream of traffic!

All completely free, permanent PR!

In addition, influencer websites usually have a high domain authority (DA). That's an SEO term and refers to how authoritative Google thinks of each site. The higher the site's DA, the easier it will be for articles on that site to show up on page 1 in Google, generating a continuous stream of "organic" traffic, meaning traffic through searches (aka googling).

Guesting is an absolute must if you want to grow quickly, and as a bestselling author, your chances of being accepted are exponentially higher. In fact, podcasters often look for guests in the bestseller lists and might even contact you directly.

For an extended video version of this chapter, you can check out the free sample from my course "Dream Clients on Autopilot" on the **Resources Page**. It is an in-depth 20-minute look at how to "guest your best."

VIDEO: How to Guest Your Best!

If you are still not convinced, let's hear Richie Norton, one of the most successful podcast "guesters" of our time (and he doesn't even have his own podcast):

"There was a month when I did over $300K in just that month. I looked at the sales and saw that more than 80% of the revenue came from being a guest on a podcast. No paid ads.

Since then, my companies have done over $1 million just from one podcast guesting show. More, of course, from the over 300 shows I've been on.

The idea is this: If you want to reach 1 million people it would be hard on your own. If you do 10 podcasts that have 100,000 people reach in a day, you can reach 1 million people in a day . . . theoretically."

How is that for OPA...?

Finding them...

How then do you find suitable blogs and podcasts to guest on?

Here are a few criteria:

1) First of all, you are looking for audiences similar to yours because you are trying to drive traffic to your business, books, and platforms. You can look through the blog posts or podcast episodes to find a match. Not just topic, but also style and personality.

2) Secondly, you want blogs and podcasts with a large, active audience. Those are pretty easy to spot:

– *Blogs:* look at the number of comments and social shares under each post. An active blog will have plenty of both and usually a lively conversation. You can also check their social media platforms.

– *Podcasts:* podcasts are often hosted on the owner's website, and you might find comments and social shares there as well. In addition, you can see the number of reviews on iTunes, number of episodes, start date, and of course, the podcaster's social media platforms.

There are no exact numbers, and it varies greatly by niche, but all these factors give you a good sense of whether this podcast or blog are worth pursuing.

3) Make sure the blog or podcast accepts guests. On blogs you will usually find a "Guest Posts" or "Work with Us" section (often in the "About" tab or footer) including submission requirements and other info. Be sure to follow those to the letter.

For podcasts, check out their episodes and see if they frequently have guests on and what type of guests.

How do you find suitable podcasts?

1) Search on iTunes or Stitcher for your niche and also under "New and Noteworthy".

2) Google your **[sub niche] + podcast** or **blog.**

3) Google your **[peer/competitor name] + podcast** or **blog** and see where they have guested. This is a shortcut and can be a great starting point since you already know that these podcasts accept guests like you.

4) Ask your existing audience for their favorite blogs and podcasts.

5) Install a Facebook Ad pixel on your site and see what influencers your visitors follow.

Landing them...

Next, it's time to pitch the blog or podcast owner. You can refer back to STEP 1, the influencer section, as the same principles and etiquette apply here.

Hopefully, you already built some relationships, which will make this a lot easier.

If not, take some time with each site or podcast. Look through their episodes and most popular blog posts. Find out what *exactly* they are looking for. What haven't they covered yet that you could write or talk about?

Find topics that will provide **massive benefit to their audience**, that will make them look good. The kind their audience will thank them for. Be that guest!

Of course, it should tie in with your business and serve as a funnel to your books, services, and products.

With podcasts you can usually keep the same topic with slight adjustments for each audience. With blogs you need to have a different topic every time. Blog owners will not accept articles that have been posted elsewhere. Not even a variation.

You can start with BuzzSumo and see what topics are currently trending in your niche. BuzzSumo will list the articles that got the most social shares for each topic and keyword. Check what other topics have been featured on that blog, especially under "Most Popular" and see if you can fill a void or elaborate further on a sub point that could use further exploration.

When you are ready, contact the owner with a personalized email. Address them by name and share something you liked about their site or podcast, something great you learned. Be genuine, because they get hundreds of requests and yours needs to stand out.

Very few wannabe guests take the time to do this step well, but it's one of the most crucial. Craft a well-written (no spelling errors) introductory email, include the above, and most of all, how you plan to add value to *their* audience. Pitch one to three topics and include any past blogs and podcasts you have guested on. Of course, mention your bestselling books and any other credentials. This is the time for name dropping!

Give them one to two weeks to respond, and then follow up. Also, keep interacting in their comments and social media as we discussed in STEP 1, and most of all, be patient.

The bigger the name, the longer it will usually take, but if you are persistent and offer a good fit for their audience, you have a good chance of eventually being accepted.

For guest blogging I found Jon Morrow's course invaluable. I already mentioned it in STEP 2. Jon is one of the most successful bloggers in the world, paid thousands of dollars per guest article, all while being paralyzed from the neck down!

Not only that - before starting his own eight-figure blog *SmartBlogger*, he served for several years as editor to some of the biggest blogs in the business, including *Copyblogger*. In other words, he was the gatekeeper who decided who got featured and who didn't!

If anyone can teach you how to land guest spots on some of the biggest publications in the world, including Forbes, the Huffington Post, and

Lifehacker, it is Jon! The course even includes a little black book with direct editor contacts of 100+ top blogs in all major niches.

All of the editors were hand picked by Jon and are fully aware of his program. They know that alumni from his training are professionally trained and ready, making acceptance a lot easier even as a newbie.

I got accepted by *Goodlife Zen* within four weeks of signing up (and that included going through the course), followed soon after by the biggest travel blog in the world, *The Planet D*, and several others.

I already mentioned how much Jon's training changed the course of my writing career and how fortunate I was to find it right at the start, before even publishing my first book.

Whether the course is for you or not depends on your situation, but I would not do this chapter justice without mentioning Jon's training as an amazing resource. You can get a 30% discount on the **Resources Page**.

John Lee Dumas and Richie Norton offer an excellent **podcast guesting course -** *PodcastGuestMastery.com* - that goes a lot more in-depth on how to structure your presentation, craft a compelling story, be memorable to an audience that has never heard of you before, and how to effectively monetize your appearances.

Get featured!

Finally, let's talk about media outreach, an alternative to guesting. There are two options. You can either:

• contact contributors of large publications such as *Inc., Entrepreneur, Psychology Today*, or the *Huffington Post*, and see if they want to write a story about you, your brand, an exciting new product or an interesting hack that you discovered

or

• you hire a PR firm to connect you.

Contributors get a lot of requests, but they also need to post regularly in most cases. Forbes contributors, for example, are required to publish one article per week! That's a lot of articles (and topics)! => A great chance for *you*!

To start, use the search function on your publication of choice. Find contributors in your niche and start reading their articles. Narrow in on a few whose style and topics best align with yours. Start commenting under their posts and social media. Check out their website and find out as much as you can.

When you are ready, pitch them a topic that they could interview you for. Don't be shy. You are a bestselling author! If your topic is of interest to their audience and you present yourself well, there is a good chance a few will say yes, either right away or down the road. Once again, it's about building relationships and having a long-term mindset.

An interesting insight into the workings of top-level contributors is shared in this article by long time Forbes contributor Josh Steimle:

How to Become a Forbes Writer

He is another influencer I love being subscribed to because he always shares amazing tips and hacks.

If you don't succeed or don't want to spend the time, you can hire a PR firm to connect you. This is very pricey. A Forbes feature can cost $3,000 and The Huffington Post around $2,000 *(paid to the PR firm for making the connection, not the writer. Top publications usually don't allow writers to accept payments for articles).*

The exposure, resulting traffic and prestige can well be worth the luxury price tag *if* you have the budget.

MWI *(run by Josh Steimle)* and **Legal Morning** are two reputable options.

Once again, for a more in-depth look at this chapter, you can check out this free video excerpt (no opt-in required - right on the resources page):

VIDEO: How to Guest Your Best!!

STEP 5:
Go Wide!

Whatcha wanna be...?

In STEP 2, we talked about *Starting from the End* when planning out your influencer strategy and one of the questions I suggested was:

As an influencer, what other platforms do you want to employ down the road? - e.g., a podcast, Youtube channel, blog, social media platform, keynote/TED, TV, etc.

Now is definitely the time to add one or two of those bad boys. Your bestselling book traffic and established audience will make this quite easy right out of the gate.

Your followers will find it exciting and cheer you on. It will be another way to hang out with you and learn cool stuff.

If you do a lot of guesting, you should also get quite a bit of evergreen traffic from those appearances. When you add another platform, you can simply update your author/guest bio and invite people over to your new cool digs. (Don't you love the internet?)

Platforms could be:

- a podcast or online radio show
- a YouTube channel
- a blog
- an online TV show
- One to two more social media platforms, in particular Instagram and Pinterest

Pinterest boards and pins are very easy to rank in Google (SEO) and can quickly open up another traffic source right there. Be sure to either learn Pinterest marketing well or hire an expert Pinterest Ninja to get you going quickly.

Same with Instagram, the ultimate influencer platform. David Chan from *Foundr Magazine* offers an amazing course on Instagram marketing. *Foundr* famously grew their following from zero to 300,000 in just ten months, and Nathan shares all his amazing hacks.

Social media marketing can be time consuming and tedious because you need to keep active and post regularly.

Your time is your most precious commodity, and you can grow a lot faster if you leverage your time.

A virtual assistant, as discussed in STEP 3, can be a welcome, fun addition to free up your time and grow your brand quickly.

Your new platforms will also open up additional monetization options such as:

- affiliate offers
- sponsorships
- selling ads
- additional product and book sales
- additional clients for your services

Bestseller Publishing will once again be the FAST TRACK method to jump start any platform — pretty much on autopilot.

COOL LITTLE HACK:

In your books, rather than just inviting people to follow you on your other platforms, a more effective way will be to link out to relevant tutorials

(YouTube), interviews (podcast) and helpful articles (blog). Since the content will be free and books are limited to some degree, readers will be grateful for the additional (free) resources and appreciate your multimedia approach.

To avoid overwhelm, I would focus on one new platform at a time, really master it and grow a following quickly before adding any more (if at all) rather than jumping around and doing five new things all at once.

I don't know about you, but I also like to enjoy life. Smell the roses, be amazed by a gorgeous sunset, and enjoy the gentle purr of a cat on my lap *(THE most important thing of all)*.

You don't need to cover everything or be present on a million platforms. Be exclusive and choose the few where you can be reached. Beyond that, have clear boundaries while keeping free time to actually *live*.

Another reason not to waste endless months trying to "wing it" somehow. Instead, learn from the best, and then FAST TRACK the process.

There are proven hacks and strategies for each platform, and unless you apply them and learn the sequence it will be very slow and difficult.

Let's have a look:

Podcast

For podcasting, John Lee Dumas and his partner Kate Erickson from the top-rated *Entrepreneur on Fire* podcast created an amazing course: *Podcaster's Paradise*. I've taken it myself, and it's awesome! On the **Resources Page** you can sign up for a free live masterclass with JLD once a month, and he will tell you all that's involved in starting and running a successful podcast. He is making 6 figures per month(!) (as publicly posted on his website), so you definitely want to listen to him.

YouTube Channel

Starting a YouTube channel is pretty easy. Making it successful, however, is not, and most new channels fail.

My *Social Media Marketing Beginner Guide* has a 10,000-word chapter on YouTube Marketing alone at a whopping 99 cents. That will give you a good first overview of what's involved and how to succeed.

In addition, these three (FREE) Top rated channels give you many hours of free advice. Happy binge watching...

Roberto Blake
Tim Schmoyer/Video Creators
Derral Eves

If you are ready to rock and want a fast track, step by step approach, you can check out Tim Schmoyer's course.

For vlogging, ***Vlog like a Boss*** by Top Vlogger Amy Schmittauer is awesome.

Blog

You should definitely have a blog on your website and occasionally write some niche relevant articles to share with your audience. Also for SEO purposes, so your site will start ranking in Google and people can find you through Google searches (aka "organic" traffic).

If you don't have a website yet - or yours could use a facelift - I recently created a **Sassyliscious Blogging Bootcamp** to take you through the basic steps, quickly and painlessly.

To successfully grow a blog audience, you can find an abundance of free tips and resources on S*martblogger*, *Problogger* and *BlogTyrant* to name just a few.

The Pro version would be *Jon's Serious Bloggers Only community* (monthly subscription).

Social Media Influencer
As discussed above.

Passive Income Bonanza!

The natural progression from books are online courses and if you get the marketing right, they can become a passive income bonanza!

As a bestselling author you have it much easier than most, because you will automatically get qualified traffic and most importantly, pre-qualified, "hot" traffic from people who already know and like you and are convinced of your expertise.

A course allows you to go much deeper, offer over-the-shoulder tutorials, and really help your readers 10X their success.

Books are a great introduction and can offer a wealth of information, but they don't compare to the depth and hands-on training you can provide in a course. It's just a whole different ball game.

That is why courses have a much higher perceived value compared to books, and that is why you can charge a *lot* more - even hundreds of dollars.

I love online courses. I take them all the time and I always learn a few new amazing things - even in topics that I thought I knew really well.

I wouldn't be here today if it hadn't been for a number of really amazing courses!

Books are great, but they can only take you so far and if an author I like offers a course, I will usually sign up right away.

It saved so much time, because I learned from the best and could instead use that extra time to write more books, grow my brand - and... travel, enjoy life, watch movies, have FUN!

Remember FUN?

It is easy to get carried away on this journey and become obsessed with making ever more money, growing ever more followers, breaking yet another record.

What good does it do though if you don't enjoy what you achieved and also have some fun along the way?

I'm sorry if I'm digressing, but I have witnessed it a number of times with friends and peers and it is rather sad to see.

Ambition takes over becoming almost an addiction - more ever more. They are nice, wonderful people, but become totally obsessed with constantly achieving more, beating yet another competitor, finding yet another hack to make money and becoming even more efficient and successful.

If that floats your boat and you feel truly fulfilled, by all means, go for it! But I can't help feeling that something is missing in that scenario, the actual reason *why* we started all this in the first place:

Fulfillment, the joy of self-expression, the simple pleasure of being alive. Freedom most of all and not having to worry about money, not slaving in a job you hate or living in a situation that crushes your spirit.

It seems the line between fulfillment and obsession is quickly crossed and rarely noticed by those who cross it. Rather sad, because life passes so quickly and can be over in just a split second.

Somehow I doubt that at the end of our journey, we will look back and cherish all the money we made or the successes we had. But rather, how fully we lived each moment, how present we were when it happened and how connected we were with those around us, and the world as a whole.

Might seem poetic and you may think it doesn't concern you, but it can happen and much faster than you think. Please forgive me for digressing and getting this little side note off my chest.

Now back to courses:

For starters, you can turn your book into a smaller course by turning your text into Powerpoint slides and recording your screen while explaining with audio.

This is easy to do with softwares like *Screenflow* (Mac) or *Camtasia* (PC) and an inexpensive pro level mike like the *AT-2100* (around $65).

The video on the **Resources Page** shows you how to record and edit within Screenflow, using both Powerpoint and your regular computer screen.

Even if you were not born with a "tech gene", you can do this.

Once you have all your videos recorded, you need a platform to host the course.

There are three main options:

1) Self host on your website - or a separate site
Requires a course theme, plus a membership plugin and a payment processor like Paypal or Stripe. While it is not terribly difficult, this setup requires a little more tech knowledge or someone to set it up for you, so might not be the best solution for everyone

2) Sign up with a Course Platform like *Teachable*
Easy to use. Just upload your videos, choose a design and Teachable will take care of sign ups, memberships and payments. Only downside: it's quite pricey and a monthly subscription. In the lower packages, Teachable will also charge a percentage on every sale.

3) Submit to Course Marketplaces like *Udemy*
Same as 2), but also a course market place. Course pricing tends to be very low and Udemy will take a commission out of every sale, but if tech stuff scares you and you want an easy, low cost introduction, Udemy can be a good option for your first course. Unlike with Teachable your course needs to pass approval to be featured on Udemy.

Launching and marketing is usually the hard part with any new course, but thanks to your bestselling books and the mailing list and Facebook group you have built and cultivated over the past few months, this should be pretty easy now. You can even create a series of smaller courses and turn them into a full academy with a monthly membership.

Courses are the natural progression from books and can massively increase your income - pretty much on autopilot.

I generate up to 10K a month of passive income from courses, to a large part from book traffic. While that is not a typical result, even a few hundred dollars or a few thousand dollars extra per month - completely on autopilot - are certainly worth the one-time effort of creating a course. Plus, you are offering your readers an additional helpful resource to achieve their goal.

Win-win for everyone!

STEP 6:
Reach for the Stars!

Take a moment to breathe and cherish everything you have already achieved so far:

- You designed a unique, irresistible brand and have started to grow a passionate following
- You published a bestselling book, probably several - maybe even a #1!
- You have been featured on a number of high level blogs and podcasts and people have started to notice your name and brand
- You have started to crush it on another platform

and...

- You have become really comfortable around "M". In fact, you are totally chill with her now! Who would have thought?

Looking back at where you started (actually not that long ago...) - doesn't that feel awesome?

More than you ever thought possible?

You have pretty much arrived! Now it's just scaling up and some more icing on the cake *(I like chocolate, how about you?)*.

If you are reading this book for the first time, remember the intro to this chapter and come back whenever you feel frustrated along the way.

This is what it will *feel* like when you have completed the first 5 steps. *This* - is what you can look forward to.

Hold that thought.

In the meantime, let's cover some more AWEsome!

Ready?

Let's do it!

In STEP 6, we'll enjoy a few more scrumptious offerings to leverage OPA and your newfound prestige and reach.

They all involve influencers pooling their resources for massive benefit to everyone involved, including their audiences.

If you become the organizer of such events, it can open a lot of doors even if you are not yet among the top influencers in your field. You will get a big step closer and be noticed by thousands who had never heard of you before.

You are really stepping onto the big stage now. You are getting included into the "clique" of top influencers and can leverage those new connections for even more high power guest appearances (see STEP 4) and media features.

And - you will massively grow both your mailing list and income.

Let's take a look:

10X OPA: Influencer Events & Bundles

Influencer events will help you greatly to:

- expand your network and become friends with major influencers
- massively grow your list
- become an influencer in your own right
- grow your income

There are three main ways to get influencers involved in your event. All massive win-wins for everyone involved, including your audiences:

#1 - Influencer Live Events

#2 - Influencer Bundles for Charity

#3 - Influencer Giveaways

Let's start with:

Influencer Live Events

I will focus on online events here and in particular, Facebook events, but you can apply these principles to any other platform.

To organize a Facebook event around your niche, start by reaching out to the major players in your industry and invite them to participate in a Facebook live session: a 30-60 minute slot where you (or someone else) will interview them about a special technique they teach or something else they are well-known for, followed by Q&A with the live audience.

Facebook live is great for that.

You could also schedule 2-3 influencers together having a lively conversation on a relevant topic and let the audience participate with questions in the comments.

Those are the two most common examples. Of course, there are more, but the point is to involve the audience and let them ask live questions and interact with each influencer.

Hugely popular and very easy for everyone to set up. Influencers tune in live via their computers and audience members can ask questions in the comments. It is good to have someone moderate those comments if you are busy interviewing.

You then schedule a whole sequence of sessions, each featuring a different influencer (or group), covering a half or full day - or even several days if you have a lot of participants.

Here is where the magic happens:

All participating influencers will invite *their* large lists to the event. Remember OPA?

Live events featuring major influencers are one very powerful way to leverage other people's audiences in a major way.

To get access to the event, attendees will need to register, that is, give _you_ their email address, which can massively grow your list in just a few days.

In addition, your profile and prestige will grow as you are featured alongside major influencers - <u>as one of</u>

<u>them</u>! An expert presenter in a sub niche that you dominate.

Thousands of people who had never heard of you before, will suddenly know your name and assume you are important and someone whose advice they should listen to. They will start checking out your books and products and from now on consider you an important influencer they should know about.

Not only that, you could even charge a nominal amount like $60 for VIP access to the complete sessions and long-term access to all recordings.

And... get this:

To massively sell that VIP package, you could offer influencers a generous affiliate commission on those $60 for every person they bring in - and even turn that into a little competition (hugely popular!).

Easily, thousands of dollars just from that - in just a day or two!

Can you see how just one event, when planned smartly and effectively, can have a multitude of benefits and - help establish you quickly as one of the main players in your industry?

Plus, once you have appeared on one event, you will get invitations to more - and also for guest appearances on podcasts, etc.

Your brand and income can massively grow with just one focused and well executed event.

And it's not that difficult to set up.

Key for success is to build relationships with at least 2-3 major influencers over time.

Please refer back to STEP 1 for influencer outreach.

A FAST TRACK hack to get a major influencer involved when you are still fairly new, is to become one of their success stories. Apply what they teach, either on their platform or in a course, and share a success story and testimonial. They will certainly notice you and now consider themselves your mentor. From there, it's pretty easy to ask them to appear in your event and they might even bring along a few of their influencer friends.

Once you have one or two, the rest will follow easily.

Even if you don't know anyone, don't be shy to ask. You are a bestselling author and you had quite a lot of success recently. You were featured in major publications and podcasts. You are an expert in a specific sub niche with unique, amazing knowledge that could greatly benefit *their* audience. Plus, It will take them very little time and effort to participate. So, apply your newly acquired marketing chops and make it palatable. It might be easier than you think.

Blog and podcast owners from your guesting adventures will also often be happy to participate. It's a great opportunity for them as well. Their following and list will grow and possibly even some affiliate income.

If you master STEP 2 and keep your books selling well long-term - which is the most important key to all this - you will have plenty of proof that you have something valuable to offer and that hanging out with you will be a good investment of their time, not a "favor".

A powerful, yet simple way to grow your audience, income and influencer status - all at once!

Influencer Bundles for Charity

Another awesome goodie!

This is how it works:

You pick a charity that you want to raise money for. Should be something with a broad appeal.

Then you invite a large number of influencers - high and mid level - to contribute one of their digital products for free or at a steep discount, as part of a large bundle.

Usually courses or eBooks, occasionally services. The bundle is sold at a low flat rate over a period of 5-10 days.

I've participated in several bundles and pricing was anywhere from $47 to $97, meaning buyers got access to *all* the courses and books for that one low price.

Why would influencers contribute free products?

Here is why - quadruple win-win!! *(numbers are flexible)*:

1 - 25% of all earnings will go to **charity**.

2 - 50% will be affiliate commissions => this will greatly motivate all participating **influencers** to heavily promote the bundle to their list (using their affiliate link).

3 - 25% are **your** earnings (on every single sale!)

4 - **Audiences** are getting an amazing bundle deal saving them hundreds - sometimes thousands - of dollars.

Influencers will be highly motivated because of:

- 50% affiliate commission on every sale they bring in
- OPA for *them* => their products are getting additional exposure to a huge, new audience
- they are supporting a good cause

OPA magic!

Bundles can quickly bring you exposure and connect you with the makers and shakers in your industry. Plus, anyone buying the bundle will end up on your mailing list - potentially thousands of new subscribers in just a few days.

You can run bundles and events several times a year with different influencers and then repeat again the following year. Once the relationships are established and you have a system in place (the first time will be the most nerve-wracking...), this can mostly be automated and handed over to a virtual assistant under your direction, turning it mostly into passive income, except for your brief participation and possibly some introductions.

The same applies to:

Influencer Giveaways

This is a modified version of influencer bundles. In this case, you would pool with a number of fellow authors in your field.

Everyone agrees to lower one of their books to 99c (or FREE) for a 3 day period and then markets that giveaway to their audience.

You create a web page with thumbnails for each book and use your Amazon affiliate links.

You can also use a platform like *Instafreebie* that makes this incredibly easy to set up. They might even promote your giveaway to their large audience of hundreds of thousands!

FREE Giveaways are for **list building.** From the thumbnail people are sent to the author's landing page where they first have to give their email address to get access to the book (eBook only, of course, not physical books).

99cent promos are usually sent to Amazon and will provide a boost in **sales and ranking** - plus, **affiliate income** for you if you are the organizer.

Both are awesome and come with the triple benefit of:

• connecting with other influencers
• broadening your audience
• growing your stature as an influencer

STEP 7:
Be the Star!

You made it! - The final STEP - Congrats!!

We have some fun goodies to explore, the final golden nuggets on your path to influencer "stardom"! The Holy Grail, both for recognition and income.

We'll start with Keynotes, TED Talks and becoming a TV Guest Expert. Then cover the highly lucrative arenas of JV webinars and High Ticket Masterminds and conclude with the passive income big boys: Softwares and Memberships.

Let's strap in!

TV, Keynotes and TED Talks

You've seen them. The TV experts who elegantly swoop in and dazzle you with their insights. Every network has their pool of core presenters with a few spontaneous additions depending on topic.

News cycles change rapidly and producers are always on the lookout for interesting new experts to call in - often on a moment's notice.

TV gigs are usually unpaid with rare exceptions for high profile guests. The thrill lies in the enormous exposure and clout you get by appearing in front of millions of viewers. That is influencer magic and can, of course, convert into additional book and product sales - or client requests.

Most importantly, TV appearances catapult you to national influencer status, rivaled in clout and prestige only by becoming a bestselling author.

To be considered, it is almost mandatory that you have a bestselling book that the host can briefly show when they introduce you. After all, they, too, have to justify to their audience why they called in *you* and not someone else.

As a "Bestselling Author" you will be way ahead of the crowd.

I admit, speaking gigs and TV appearances were not something I was ever interested in. I had enough live thrills in my music days and now enjoy a free schedule with mostly passive income while traveling the world at my own pace.

No to worry though, I'm not leaving you dry: for this chapter, I collected a few awesome resources that will show you the step-by-step on how to get from A to Z.

For TV appearances, this excellent article by Peter Shankman who has appeared as a guest expert on national television many times lays out the main steps, who to talk to (and who not) and even the email templates to send when you first approach producers:

How to be a Guest Expert on any Television News Program (Resources Page)

Keynotes & TED Talks

Another fun addition! And definitely furthering your influencer status.

If you like performing, entering the arena of high paying speaking gigs ($10,000K and up) will be another major step in this phase (and possibly much earlier depending on your circumstances).

You established yourself as an influencer. You can show amazing results, both for yourself and through testimonials from your students and readers. You have great case studies to share and a tried and tested method that brings results.

Now is the time to share your awesomeness with large audiences and add another active income stream to the mix.

Not just through your speaking fees, but also through the books and products you can sell at these events - often in substantial numbers!

How to book them?

Speaking gigs have different levels: paid and unpaid. Some allow you to sell books and products, others don't. Some book you directly, others via so-called "Speakers Bureaus".

Patrick Schwerdtfeger, a top keynote and motivational speaker, shares this massive in-depth article and a 30 min. video to show you the way:

How to become a Keynote Speaker

TED Talks are the Gold Standard for public speaking. Since TED wants "ideas worth sharing, the chance of your talk going viral makes it the modern equivalent of the printing press" as Fia Fasbinder writes in her excellent article on INC.:

Want to get on the TED stage? Here's How

While getting featured on TED is usually reserved to world famous authorities, you can get a foot in the door with TEDx.

TEDx are independent TED like conferences, organized locally all around the world, and have made it a lot easier to be featured. Quite a few TEDx talks have gone viral and were then added to the main

TED site, so the potential for worldwide exposure is huge.

TEDx speaker Jonathan Li shares the four main steps to get yourself booked:

4 Easy Steps to get you on TEDx Talks

JV Webinars & High Ticket Masterminds

To continue widening your authority & income, JV Webinars and High Ticket Masterminds are the next logical step:

#1 - JV Webinars

If you have a large, responsive mailing list, JV Webinars can be pure gold. "JV" stands for "joint venture" and works as follows *(very different from offline Joint Venture partnerships!)*:

You partner with another influencer or product creator and it can work both ways:

• them presenting their product to your audience
or
• you presenting your products (usually a premium course or software) to their large audience

In both cases, you split the revenue from sales, which can be huge with large, active lists.

Followers are invited to a "Free Training Webinar" where they will learn an amazing new way to grow their income, audience and brand - or whatever your audience wants to learn.

You definitely need an awesome hook and a great headline.

The training should last 45 min to an hour and really be actual, valuable training, not a sales pitch.

Be generous, give a lot and share some amazing hacks that will leave listeners pumped for more. Even if they don't buy, they should walk away satisfied and excited about what they've learned.

Don't worry if not everyone buys. You don't need that many sales to make this profitable, especially with premium courses of $1000+.

Even just 30 sales - which is not impossible if you get several hundred people attending - would be $30,000(!) for just one hour of talking!!

Yep, that's right.

If you split with your JV partner, that still leaves you with $15,000 - just like that!

Whether it is *their* list/product or yours.

You can see now:

1) how important and valuable a large, active list can be. Not just to sell your own products, but to sell other people's products for JV commissions - while - offering your audience some awesome new information and resources. Never forget that aspect and carefully select who you feature. Your audience will trust your recommendations and you worked very hard to earn that trust.

2) how important it is to build great relationships with peers and influencers over time, because finding JV partners will be a lot easier when people already know you and your work. When they trust your expertise and enjoy hanging out with you.

OPA can make you massive amounts of money with relatively little effort IF you put in the initial work first:

• grow multiple income streams
• grow a portfolio of awesome products (books, courses & services)
• grow a massive & active mailing list and community
• grow relationships with influencers and peers

IMPORTANT:

Selling in a webinar is not easy and many people get uncomfortable when they have to switch from teaching to selling.

From my own experience - and I LOVE webinars - I can say:

You need a great script! For the sales part that is.

There are tried and tested transitions with exact wording that you can simply follow. How to structure your overall webinar, when and how to make the transition, what to say and how to share your product.

Once you have done a few, this becomes a lot easier and you will suffer less from Impostor Syndrome. All it takes is a proven script and some practice, and you can turn webinars into an amazing money making machine.

Both live and evergreen.

As an author, you can invite readers to a free webinar training as your lead magnet - right from within your book. You give them awesome training that complements what you teach in the book and at the end you let them know of an additional training option for those who would like to learn more. Simple.

And on autopilot!

This you record once - or you use the recording of an earlier live webinar - and the rest is automated, together with an autoresponder email sequence to follow up.

To do this successfully, you _need_ expert training.

Russell Brunson who I mentioned in the beginning, is one of the most successful marketers in the world and built his company Clickfunnels into a 100 Million Dollar company over just a few years. He is an absolute master at webinars with a phenomenal conversion rate and his "Perfect Webinar" script is one of the best in the business.

You can start with a FREE chart and DVD explaining the process. Yes, an actual _physical_ DVD that Russell will mail you to your home anywhere in the world. You just pay for shipping...

Remember "Free + Shipping"...? - The following is a prime example of how to expertly start a funnel. If you want to see a true master in action, sign up on the Resources Page and watch how he does it:

High Ticket Masterminds

Last but certainly not least, you can now offer a high ticket mastermind. Meaning you take applications for:

• a few limited spots of premium one-on-one coaching

plus

• membership in an exclusive VIP group of students, each of them paying an annual fee of $5,000, $10,000, $25,000 or even more.

WOW!

Shocking right?

But think of it this way:

If your expertise and connections can bring someone *massive* results, there will usually be a few who can afford - and are pumped and excited - to pay such a substantial amount for your personal time.

The connections and influence you have built up until now, can then massively fast track someone else's success and the increased earnings will be well worth the luxury price tag. Plus, it is usually a tax deductible marketing expense *(confirm with your CPA)*.

Softwares & Memberships

On the passive income side there are two major areas. How passive will depend on how much you still want to be involved beyond the occasional "office hour" or Facebook appearance.

Content and customer support can largely be handled by a well trained, enthusiastic staff while you keep the overall direction, and occasionally provide content or appear live.

Jon Morrow's *Serious Bloggers Only* monthly membership course is such an example while Sean Ogle from *Location Rebel* still runs everything himself together with an awesome operations manager named Liz.

You can also partner with several other influencers and share management and content. *Fizzle* is a great example for this type of membership program.

It is a personal decision and all are awesome communities that are well worth their price.

Memberships & Subscriptions

This is where the big money and long-term financial freedom lies!

It takes significant clout and community building to get people to commit to a monthly subscription/membership of say $25, $45 or more.

Once you do and have even 100 people sign up, that becomes $2500 per month (or higher) - month after month - until someone unsubscribes.

Effective examples can be:

- *Training Academies*: rather than selling your info in one course, you give members access to the course (or several smaller courses) with a monthly subscription that also includes direct support via a Facebook group. Again, support can be handled by someone else: a topnotch expert who will focus exclusively on this program and either gets a nice salary from you or becomes a partner. If your topic requires a lot of ongoing support and updates, this can be a better option than a one-time course payment.

- *Communities for Collaboration:* a community offering blackboards for collaboration, accountability partners and gigs. Often in connection with a course and limited to only students of that course. An example is John Lee Dumas' *Podcaster's Paradise* which goes in tandem with his podcasting course. The program offers lively forums, blackboards and monthly training webinars.

Memberships are the Holy Grail of passive income and can be outsourced to a large degree while *you* focus on growing your business and other ventures. You still remain present with occasional appearances and guidance on the overall direction, but you are not running the day to day which can become exhausting.

Softwares

I mentioned apps in a previous chapter and softwares are another highly lucrative and potentially recurring income opportunity. The 10X version of apps really!

Is there a functionality in your field that has been frustrating and time consuming? Could a software solve that problem?

Obviously, you wouldn't create the software yourself, but hire an experienced programmer to code and develop according to your specifications.

Softwares come with high up-front costs as developers are expensive. Plus, it will usually take several months for development and testing and can come with quite a share of frustrations.

You will also need expert tech support once you launch, to iron out the initial bugs and support customers along the way.

Most importantly, you need to know how to market that bad boy - so definitely not a beginner strategy.

By now though, you should have a large, active list and community of fans. You will be well connected with influencers that you can invite for JVs and affiliate partnering. You will have the crucial ingredients in place.

You will also know your market and how to research winning products - and - how to run a successful launch that ties your amazing software into your overall brand.

Ideally, you make your software a monthly recurring subscription for long-term passive income streams.

And - you can offer an affiliate program to spread the word quickly and get new customers on autopilot.

Next Steps

WOW!

Take a breath...

You made it to the end!

Thanks for sticking with me and allowing me to share all this massive information with you!

I hope you feel inspired and *can't wait* to take action and plan out the next 6-12 months <u>right now</u>! You know now what to do.

I also hope we dispelled a lot of fears and apprehensions as well as all the myths that tell you that it's not possible and you could never do it.

No matter who you are and what you do, you *can* make a difference in the world and inspire others to go beyond what they ever thought possible.

Step by step, continuously and with a clear plan in sight now.

You can **do** it and I'd love to hear about your influencer adventures in our awesome, friendly Facebook group. You can head on over right here: **SassyZenGirl.Group**

NEXT STEPS:

#1 - Watch the **training video** if you haven't already and then get started with your first book. We'll support you in the group and cheer you on - and - also look forward to your support.

#2 - Go through the book again and create an action plan and timeline (6-12 months).

#3 - Bookmark the **Resources Page** with all the tools and tips mentioned in this book (no optin required).

#4 - Finally - ***PLEASE... :)*** - if you enjoyed this book, it would be **AWEsome** if you could...

... leave a quick review on Amazon.

It only takes a minute and would mean a LOT!!

You can also share this pink baby on Goodreads if that's one of your digs...:) - Thank you so very much - YOU ROCK!!

A Sassyliscious Goodbye for now, but hopefully "Auf Wiedersehen" very soon...

To your SUCCESS (+ FUN & ADVENTURE...!!)

Gundi Gabrielle
SassyZenGirl.com
InfluencerFastTrack.com

About the Author

Gundi Gabrielle, aka *SassyZenGirl*, loves to explain complex matters in an easy to understand, fun way. Her *"The Sassy Way...when you have NO CLUE!!"* series has helped thousands around the world conquer the jungles of internet marketing with humor, simplicity and some sass.

A 10-time #1 Bestselling Author, Entrepreneur and former Carnegie Hall conductor, Gundi employs marketing chops from all walks of life and loves to help her readers achieve their dreams in a practical, fun way. Her students have published multiple #1 Bestsellers outranking the likes of Tim Ferris, John Grisham, Hal Elrod and Liz Gilbert.

When she is not writing books or enjoying a cat on her lap (or both), she is passionate about exploring the world as a Digital Nomad, one awesome adventure at a time.

She has no plans of settling down anytime soon.

SassyZenGirl.com
SassyZenGirl.Group
DreamClientsOnAutopilot.com

Instagram.com/SassyZenGirl
Youtube.com/c/SassyZenGirl
Facebook.com/SassyZenGirl
Twitter.com/SassyZenGirl

More SassyZenGirl Books:

#1 Bestselling
BEGINNER INTERNET MARKETING
Series

#1 Bestseller

ZEN TRAVELLER BALI

Explore the "real" Bali...
the quiet, magical parts
- away from the tourist crowds....

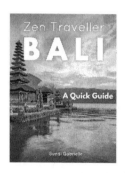

More Zen Traveller guides following soon:
New Zealand, South Africa, Andalusia, Dubai, Namibia
among others.....

#1 Bestseller

TRAVEL for FREE

How to score FREE
Flights, Rental Cars & Accommodations,
dramatically reduce Airfares,
Get paid to Travel &
START a DIGITAL NOMAD BIZ
you can run from anywhere
in the world!

Made in the USA
Lexington, KY
04 November 2018